Roberto Repole

THE DREAM OF A GOSPEL-INSPIRED CHURCH

Pope Francis' Ecclesiology

LIBERIA EDITRICE VATICANA

Published in Australia by

© Copyright 2019 Coventry Press

Coventry Press
33 Scoresby Road
Bayswater Vic. 3153
Australia

Original title: *El Evangelio de la Misericorida en espiritu de discernimiento. La etica social del papa Francisco*

Translated into English by Salesians of Don Bosco of the Province of Mary Help of Christians of Australia and The Pacific

ISBN 9780987643193

© Copyright 2017 - Libreria Editrice Vaticana
00120 Città del Vaticano
Tel. 06.698.81032 - Fax 06.698.84716
commerciale.lev@spc.va

All rights reserved. Other than for the purposes and subject to the conditions prescribed under the *Copyright Act*, no part of this publication may be reproduced, stored in a retrieval system, or transmitted in any form or by any means, electronic, mechanical, photocopying, recording or otherwise, without the prior permission of the publisher.

Cataloguing-in-Publication entry is available from the National Library of Australia http:/catalogue.nla.gov.au/.

Printed in Australia

www.coventrypress.com.au

SERIES
THE THEOLOGY OF POPE FRANCIS

- Jurgen Werbick: *God's weakness for humankind.* Pope Francis' view of God

- Lucio Casula: *Faces, gestures and places.* Pope Francis' Christology

- Peter Hünermann: *Human beings according to Christ today.* Pope Francis' Anthropology

- Roberto Repole: *The dream of a gospel-inspired Church.* Pope Francis' Ecclesiology

- Carlos Galli: *Christ, Mary, the Church and the peoples.* Pope Francis' Mariology

- Santiago Madrigal Terrazas: *'Unity Prevails over Conflict'.* Pope Francis' Ecumenism

- Aristide Fumagalli: *Journeying in love.* Pope Francis' Moral Theology

- Juan Carlos Scannone: *The Gospel of Mercy in the spirit of discernment.* Pope Francis' Social Ethics

- Marinella Perroni: *Kerygma and prophecy.* Pope Francis' Biblical Hermeneutics

- Piero Coda: *'The Church is the Gospel'.* At the sources of Pope Francis' theology

- Marko Ivan Rupnik: *According to the Spirit.* Spiritual theology on the move with Pope Francis' Church

ABBREVIATIONS

AAS	*Acta Apostolicae Sedis*
AG	*Ad Gentes*
AL	*Amoris Laetitia*
CD	*Christus Dominus*
DV	*Dei Verbum*
EG	*Evangelii Gaudium*
EN	*Evangelii Nuntiandi*
EV	*Enchiridion Vaticanum*
GS	*Gaudium et Spes*
LF	*Lumen Fidei*
LG	*Lumen Gentium*
LS	*Laudato Si'*
MeM	*Misericordia et Misera*
MV	*Misericordiae Vultus*

PREFACE TO THE SERIES

From the time of his first appearance in St Peter's Square on the evening of his election, it was more than clear that Francis' pontificate would be adopting a new style. His modest apparel, calling himself the Bishop of Rome, asking the people to pray for him – in the 'deafening silence' of a packed square – and greeting them with a simple '*buonasera*' (good evening) … these were all eloquent signs of the fact that there was a change taking place in the way the Pope related to people, and thus in the 'language' used.

The gestures and words that have followed from that occasion only confirm and strengthen this first impression. Indeed, it could be said that over the ensuing years, the image of the papacy has been decidedly transformed, involving a change that affects homilies, addresses and documents promulgated as well.

As could be predicted, this has generated divergent opinions, especially regarding his teaching. While many have in fact welcomed his magisterium with enthusiasm and deep interest, sensing the fresh wind of the gospel, some others have approached it in a more detached way and, at times, with suspicion. There has been no lack of more absolute views, even going as far as to doubt the existence of a theology in Francis' teaching.

A summary judgement of this kind could come from the very different backgrounds of Francis and his predecessor, Benedict XVI. The latter, we know, has been one of the most outstanding and important theologians of the twentieth century and undoubtedly relied on his personal theological development in his rich papal magisterium. We have not yet fully appreciated, nor will we cease to appreciate, the depth of this magisterium. What Bergoglio has behind him, on the other hand, is his long and deep-rooted experience as a religious and a pastor.

However, this does not mean that his magisterium is without a theology. The fact that he was not mostly, or only, a 'professional' theologian does not mean that his magisterium is not supported by a theology. Were this the case, we could say that, strictly speaking, the majority of his predecessors were without a theology, given that Ratzinger represents the exception rather than the rule.

In any case, the fact that we can discuss the theological significance of Francis' magisterium, as well as the fact that, very often, some of his highly evocative and very immediate expressions have been so abused as to rob them of their profundity – in the journalistic as well as the ecclesial ambit – makes the response of this series, which I have the honour of presenting, a significant one.

By drawing on the competence and rigorous study of theologians of proven worth, coming from diverse contexts, the series has sought to research the theological thinking which supports the Pope's teaching. It explores its roots, its freshness, and its continuity with earlier magisterium.

The result can be found in the eleven volumes which make up this series with its simple and direct title: 'The Theology of Pope Francis'.

They can be read independently of one another, obviously; they have been written by individual authors independently of each other. Nevertheless, the hope is that a reading of the entire series would not only be a valuable aid for grasping the theology upon which Francis' teaching is based, in the various theological fields of knowledge, but also an introduction to the key points of his thinking and teaching overall.

The intention, then, is not one of 'apologetics', and even less so is it to add further voices to the many already speaking about the Pope. The aim is to try to see, and to help others to see, what theological thinking Francis bases himself on and expresses, in such a fresh way in his teaching.

Among the many discoveries the reader could make in reading these volumes, would certainly be that of observing how so much of the beneficial freshness of the Council's teaching flows into Francis' magisterium. This is true both of the theological preparation he has had, and of what has followed from it. Given that it is perhaps still too soon for all this wealth to become common patrimony, peacefully and fully received by everyone, it should be no surprise that the Pope's teaching is sometimes not immediately understood by everyone.

By the same token, a point of no return has been reached in Francis' teaching, one that recent theology and the Council have both taught: that doctrine cannot be something extraneous to so-called pastoral theology and ministry. The truth that the Church is called to watch over is the truth of Christ's gospel, which needs to be communicated to the women and men of every time and place. This is why the task of the ecclesial magisterium must also be one of favouring this communication of the gospel. Hence, theology can never be reduced to a dry, desk-bound exercise, disconnected from the life of the people of God and its mission. This mission is that the women and men of every age encounter the perennial and inexhaustible freshness of Jesus' gospel.

Over these years there have been those who have heard some of Francis' own critical statements regarding theology or theologians, and have concluded that he holds it and them in low esteem. Perhaps a more detailed study of the Pope's teaching, such as offered by this series, could also be helpful for showing that, while we always need to be critical of a theology that loses its vital connection to the living faith of the Church, it is also essential to have a theology which takes up the task of thinking critically about this very faith, and doing so with 'creative fidelity', so that it may continue to be proclaimed.

Francis' teaching is certainly not lacking in a theology of this kind; and a theology of the kind is certainly one much desired by a magisterium such as his, which so wants God's mercy to continue to touch the minds and hearts of the women and men of our time.

Editor-in-chief
ROBERTO REPOLE

CONTENTS

Abbreviations 4
Preface to the Series 5

Chapter 1

The Primacy of the Gospel 21

    1. De Trinitate Ecclesia 21

    2. The gospel of mercy 27

        2.1. The gospel cannot be reduced to an idea 31

        2.2. The gospel that needs to reach us 33

        2.3. The gospel that calls for free adherence and conversion 35

    3. The Church as mother. The importance of ecclesial mediation 37

Chapter 2

The 'Holy Faithful People of God' 45

    1. People of God: return to a central category 45

        1.1. God chooses and saves a people 49

        1.2. The universal scope of the Church ... 50

        1.3. Equal dignity and shared responsibility of all Christians 52

        1.4. Popular, not populist. The challenge of a mystical fraternity .. 55

2. *'Circumdata varietate' and 'the coat of many colours'* 58

   2.1. Reference to the 'theology of the people' 59

   2.2. The people in the peoples 61

3. *Sensus fidei. A new and provocative interpretation* 64

   3.1. The meaning of divine things and the possibility of expressing them 66

   3.2. Popular piety, its value and limitations 68

Chapter 3

An Extroverted Church: A Church that Exists for Others 73

1. *We are all missionary disciples: those who proclaim and the gospel that is proclaimed* 76

2. *Mission and pastoral conversion* 80

3. *Lay involvement* 84

4. *A style that is also its content* 87

5. *The prophetic dimension of proclamation: denouncing practical relativism* 91

Chapter 4

The Necessary Reform 95
    1. Synodality and overcoming a universalist view of Church 97
    2. Episcopal conferences and intermediate collegiality 103
    3. The Papacy and the Synod of bishops 106

Epilogue 111

Being Involved in the Dream To Remain Faithful to the Gospel 111

PROLOGUE
SO A DREAM MAY BE PRESERVED AND CAN GROW

In an undoubtedly evocative way, one could say that at the beginning, the Church was able to 'set out into the deep' thanks to a dream.

We know that dreams in the Bible are often places where God shows himself, lets his will be known, points the way and reveals new paths. From Joseph the Patriarch, the 'lord of dreams' to Joseph the 'Just man', father and custodian of Jesus, the Scriptures abound in accounts of dreams in which God comes close to people and opens up their future.

A vision is recounted in the *Acts of the Apostles*. It borders on a dream through which Peter understands how the Church cannot be confined to the group of Judaeo-Christians but is meant for everyone, because God does not show partiality. In Acts 10, in fact, it says that Peter fell into a trance – this corresponded to the vision Cornelius, a pagan, had had in Caesarea. Peter, who was in Joppa, had gone up onto the roof to pray at midday and was hungry. While his food was being prepared for him he had a vision. The Author of Acts tells us that

> He became hungry and wanted something to eat; and while it was being prepared, he fell into a trance. He saw the heaven opened and something like a large sheet coming down,

> being lowered to the ground by its four corners. In it were all kinds of four-footed creatures and reptiles and birds of the air. Then he heard a voice saying, "Get up, Peter; kill and eat." But Peter said, "By no means, Lord; for I have never eaten anything that is profane or unclean." The voice said to him again, a second time, "What God has made clean, you must not call profane." This happened three times, and the thing was suddenly taken up to heaven (acts 10:10-16).

The vision would not only tell him that by now there was no difference between clean and unclean foods. It would become ever clearer to Peter through this vision and the request to go to Cornelius' home, and to the primitive Christian community, that gentiles too were to be welcomed into the unity of the Church.[1] Peter would not only enter Cornelius' home, but would proclaim the gospel there and, through baptism, would see that he and his family were welcomed into the community.

This was a crucial 'dream' for a better understanding of how Jesus Christ is the 'Lord of all' (Acts 10:36) and how, as a consequence, the Church is not a a little clique or sect for some. On the contrary, it is a place of reconciliation and unity for Jews and Gentiles or, in other words, for the whole of humanity (cf. Eph 2:11-22).

The episode would be so crucial for the future of the Church and for understanding this reality, that it has been

---

1 Cf. *Gli Atti degli apostoli* (commentary by G Stählin), Paideia, Brescia 1973, 271-272.

possible to speak not just of Cornelius' 'conversion' but of Peter's and the original Christian community's too: 'With the baptism of Cornelius and his family "it is religion itself that is being redefined."'[2] Peter's 'dream', then, was crucial for the Church to discover itself and become what it was destined to be.

In likewise evocative terms, one could say that across two thousand years of history, the Church has always needed Christians who are able to re-activate this same dream in order to remain faithful to their proper identity as time passes and situations change.

So we should not be in any way astonished that today too, Pope Francis often lets us know what his vision of the Church is, and what road or what direction we should be encouraged to take. He often goes back to the image of the dream or to metaphors and language close to this and which are able to express desires, hopes, processes to be put in place … as he loves to often say.[3]

This is the kind of language he has used since the day after his election. Recounting how he came to choose the name Francis and explaining how one of the reasons he had taken this name could be found in the attention St Francis paid to the poor, he said: 'Ah, how I would like a poor

---

2 SB BEVANS – RP SCHROEDER, *Teologia per la missione oggi. Costanti nel contesto*, Queriniana, Brescia 2010, 60. Cf. also pp. 58-59.

3 This is how Gronchi interpreted the Pope's first document: cf. M GRONCHI, *Il sogno di papa Francesco*, in M GRONCHI – R REPOLE, *Il dolce stil nuovo di papa Francesco*, Messaggero, Padova 2015, 11-48.

Church for the poor!'[4] The same kind of language can be found in *Evangelii Gaudium* (*EG*) where, on the basis of the underlying theme characterizing this Apostolic Exhortation the Pope says: 'I dream of a "missionary option", that is, a missionary impulse capable of transforming everything, so that the Church's customs, ways of doing things, times and schedules, language and structures can be suitably channeled for the evangelization of today's world rather than for her self-preservation.'[5] At the 5th National Congress of the Italian Church, the Pope once again returned to words recalling the notion of dream: 'I prefer a restless Italian Church' he said, 'ever closer to the abandoned, the forgotten, the imperfect. I would like a glad Church with a mother's face, that understands, accompanies, caresses. You too dream of this Church, believe in her, innovate with freedom.'[6]

It is the tenor of this latter address (we could add many others to it), during which Francis invited the Italian Church to be and live according to the mind of Jesus Christ – where humility, disinterest and beatitude stand out – that leads me to say that Pope Francis' dream, is basically a very simple one and, because of this, rather unsettling: one could immediately say that it is about the *dream of a gospel-inspired Church*.

---

[4] FRANCIS, *Audience granted to representatives of the media*, Saturday 16 March 2013.

[5] *EG*, no. 27.

[6] FRANCIS, *Meeting with representatives of the 5th Congress of the Italian Church*, Santa Maria del Fiore Cathedral, Florence, Tuesday 10 November 2015.

This means a Church constantly able to face up to itself, its life, its choices and structures, with the freshness of the gospel, knowing all too well that the gospel is a treasure given to the Church, guarded and transmitted by it so that all human beings may be able to live by it. A gospel-inspired Church, then, is a Church called to constantly measure itself by the breadth and richness of the Gospel of Christ. Thus the adjective 'restless' is in no way foreign to expressing its constitution. Obviously it is not the restlessness of someone with an 'open identity' who might go in any direction, as we will see later; but it is the restlessness which ultimately comes from the Church at the service of that one Lord, who is always greater and beyond her and who is, indeed, the Lord of the cosmos and of people.

It would, however, falsify reality to say that Francis' dream represents an absolute beginning. Just as there is the danger of neutralizing his magisterium by making him appear to be poor in thinking or theology, so there is the opposite danger of exalting his magisterium as if it were a teaching that had broken free of the path taken by previous magisterium and Church history.

The desire to see and study the ecclesiological vision underlying Pope Francis' chief documents and interventions is a way of saying, in an outright and succinct way, that we are faced with a new phase of reception of ecclesiological teaching as expressed by Vatican II.

Francis is the first pope not to have taken part in the Council's work. However, he is fully a son of the Council and the ecclesial renewal which began with it. Seeing his gestures, reading his documents and listening to his interventions reveals a view of the Church which is deeply rooted in the perspectives brought about by the last Council, the rich theology which preceded and then followed it. Moreover, it is the Pope himself who tells us both explicitly and implicitly that Vatican II is the background against which to see his pontificate and magisterium. In this regard it should not go unobserved that Francis tells us, in the Bull of Indiction for the Extraordinary Jubilee of Mercy, that he chose 8 December as the date for the opening of the Holy Year since it was the fiftieth anniversary of the closing of the Council.[7] Nor can we forget to mention how, in *EG* 17, speaking of offering some guidelines to encourage and guide the Church in a new phase of evangelization, he goes back to the teaching of the Dogmatic Constitution *Lumen Gentium*.

This does not mean that the views offered by Francis lack a certain originality. On the contrary, we can say that they echo the place from which Jorge Bergoglio comes, the 'end of the world' he referred to when he first appeared in public on the evening of his election to the papacy. They also

7   "I will open the Holy Door on the fiftieth anniversary of the closing of the Second Vatican Ecumenical Council. The Church feels a great need to keep this event alive. With the Council, the Church entered a new phase of her history. The Council Fathers strongly perceived, as a true breath of the Holy Spirit, a need to talk about God to men and women of their time in a more accessible way. The walls which for too long had made the Church a kind of fortress were torn down and the time had come to proclaim the Gospel in a new way. It was a new phase of the same evangelization that had existed from the beginning" FRANCIS, *Misericordiae Vultus. Bull of Indiction for the Extraordinary Jubilee of Mercy*, 11 April 2015, no. 4.

bear the legacy of a particular version of Latin American theology which goes under the name of 'theology of the people',[8] as well as that special spirituality which had already been a response to modernity, which is Ignatian spirituality.[9]

This originality, nevertheless, needs to be seen in the context of Vatican II, as we have said, and in this regard it would seem appropriate to mention that reception of the Council has entered a new phase with Francis. Furthermore,

---

8   Carlos Galli says that 'la gran novedad del pontificado de Francisco incluye la pequeña novedad de un primer conocimiento de aportes de la teología argentina (The great novelty of Francis' pontificate includes the smaller novelty of a first understanding of the contribution of Argentinian theology)', CM GALLI, *EL 'retorno del Pueblo de Dios misonero. Un concepto-simbolo de la eclesiología del Concilio a Francisco*, in VR AXCUY – JC CAMAÑO – CM GALLI (eds.). *La eclesiología del Concilio Vaticano II,* Agape Libros, Buenos Aires 2015, 405-471, 426. The theology he refers to is the so-called 'theology of the people' one of whose first and most important exponents was the Italian-Argentinian thinker Lucio Gera (1924-2012): cf. 424-431.

9   It is in this sense that we share what has been said by Piero Coda, that Pope Francis "... in some ways embodies the renewal promoted by Vatican II: he is the first non-European Pope who gives back to the universal Church the abundant and fresh results the Council's teaching brought to the continent of hope, Latin America; he is the first Pope to offer the whole Church a program based on the richness of the charism of St Ignatius of Loyola, the saint of modernity, and of St Francis of Assisi, the saint in whom the *forma Evangelii* is proposed as the *forma* Ecclesiae", P CODA, *Il Concilio della Misericordia. Sui sentieri del Vaticano II*, Città Nuova, Rome 2015, 21. Regarding the weight that Ignatian spirituality carries in Francis' theology, it is useful to look at the study by A COZZI, *La verità di Dio e dell'uomo in Cristo. Il teologico e l'antropologico nella cristologia di J. Bergoglio*, in A COZZI – R REPOLE – G PIANA, *Papa Francesco. Quale teologia?* (afterword by Gianfranco Ravasi), Cittadella, Assisi 2016, 13-67

the very fact that there is a pope coming from Latin America who can draw on the experience of that Church as well as the theology that has been developed there is already a first fruit of the Council if it is true, as Karl Rahner used say, that one of the more novel aspects of Vatican II is a Church that has become worldwide.[10] On the other hand, the pastoral nature of the Council and the 'updating' that took place with it, require a 'creative fidelity', especially at the level of ecclesiological reflection. We will be faithful to what the Council was, and said, if we continue to rethink the Church in the light of revelation and the gospel, as it is in the world and in the 'worlds' of today: this is a clear concern in the entire magisterium of the current pope.

Having said that, it is clear that we should not be looking for a systematic vision of things in Francis' teaching, as, of course, we cannot nor should we go looking for that in the teaching of all his predecessors. One clear ecclesiological perspective, though, can be found in his teaching, and explaining it as best we can and giving it the best possible reasoning is the main task of this essay.

---

10 Cf. K RAHNER, *Interpretazione teologica fondamentale del Concilio Vaticano II*, in K RAHNER, *Sollecitudine per la Chiesa. Nuovi saggi VIII*, Paoline, Rome 1982, 343-361. Cf. in the same volume, K RAHNER, *Il significato permanente del Concilio Vaticano II*, 362-380.

Chapter 1
THE PRIMACY OF THE GOSPEL

1. *De Trinitate Ecclesia*

As a professor of theology and colleague, the illustrious theologian Joseph Ratzinger was able to disagree and take his distance from some positions of Karl Rahner's best-known student, Johann Baptist Metz. In more recent years, when he was by then Prefect of the Congregation for the Doctrine of the Faith, Cardinal Ratzinger expressed words of praise for the conference that Metz gave in 1993, as he was leaving his Chair at Münster. What his old colleague was praising was the emphasis placed by Metz on the centrality for the European context today of the great question of God: an issue that even risked being shielded, so to speak, by so much talk about the Church. What Metz somehow ended up denouncing in that speech was the fact that Vatican II had only picked up half of the legacy left by Vatican Council I. The latter, in fact, had not only raised the ecclesiological issue but, more radically, the question of God, while the last Council had spoken of God as proclaimed by the Church.

This praise of Metz' address was Cardinal Ratzinger's way of expressing his basic thesis regarding the last Council which he summed up as follows: ' ... Vatican II clearly sought to place side by side and subordinate discourse about the Church to discourse about God; it sought to offer an ecclesiology in a properly theological sense, but reception of the Council has thus far overlooked this qualifying characteristic, preferring to make individual ecclesiological claims ...'[1]

One can object to his judgement on reception, as well as to the positions taken by Cardinal Ratzinger in that text on various ecclesiological questions. No one can fail to note, however, that a complete reading of the Council's *corpus* leads us to acknowledge how the Council really did enrich ecclesiological discourse from a christological and, ultimately, theological perspective.

Referring to the opening paragraph of *Lumen Gentium* (*LG*), the then Cardinal Ratzinger could therefore rightly say that

> the first sentence of the Constitution on the Church makes it clear that the Council does not think of the Church as a reality closed within itself, but sees it beginning from Christ: 'Christ is the Light of nations. Because this is so, this Sacred Synod gathered together in the Holy Spirit eagerly desires, by proclaiming the Gospel to every creature, to bring the light of Christ to all men ...' In the background we recognize the image found in the theology of the fathers who see the Church as the moon which does not have its own light but refers to the light of

---

[1] J. RATZINGER, *L'ecclesiologia della costituzione* Lumen Gentium, in J. RATZINGER, *La comunione nella Chiesa*, San Paolo, Cinisello Balsamo (MI) 2010, 129-161, 132.

> Christ, its sun. Ecclesiology shows up as being dependent on Christology, is tied to it. However, since no one can correctly talk about Christ, about the Son without at the same time talking about the Father, and since one cannot correctly talk about the Father and the Son without being in an attitude of listening to the Holy Spirit, the christological view of the Church necessarily broadens into being a trinitarian ecclesiology. Discourse on the Church is discourse about God, and this is how it should be.[2]

The first and most important shift the Council made at the ecclesiological level is undoubtedly conveyed by the first chapter of *LG* in which the mystery of the Church is presented, the Church which owes its existence to God's free self-emergence: the Father's universal plan of salvation manifested in the sending of his Son, which occurs through the gift of the Spirit (*LG* 2-4). This perspective is summed up in a quote from Cyprian placed at the conclusion to no. 4: 'a people made one with the unity of the Father, the Son and the Holy Spirit.' This quote serves to remind us that the trinitarian God is the foundation of the Church. It is relevant to say, then, that the first great turning point made by Vatican II where ecclesiology is concerned, is of a methodological kind before being one of content.[3] It consists

---

2 *Ibidem*, 147-148

3 Cf. A Antón, *Ecclesiologia postconciliare: speranze, risultati, prospettive*, in R Latourelle (ed.), *Vaticano II. Bilancio e prospettive venticinque anni dopo (1962-1987)*, vol. 1, Cittadella, Assisi 1988, 361-388, 365. On the importance of this shift by the Council and

of thinking about how the Church has its foundation, its end, its most profound *raison d'être* in God, who constantly dwells within it and from whom it lives.[4]

It would be misleading to talk about Francis' ecclesiology without especially highlighting how, for him too, the Church owes its existence to God who has fully communicated himself in Christ and the gift of the Spirit and how it lives through him and directs itself to him. Some of his words, loaded with metaphor, risk becoming slogans – at the level of journalism or even in ecclesiastical jargon – when stripped of their profundity; something that happens, inevitably, when this theological anchoring of the Church is not stressed. Think, for example, of phrases like 'the Church going forth', 'the Church of the peripheries', 'the Church as a field hospital', pastors who need 'to have the smell of the sheep' ...

It is sufficient to listen to some of his homilies to be aware of the fact that the Church has meaning for Francis inasmuch as it is especially the place where God acts and because it is completely in reference to Christ and has the Spirit dwelling in it. This is the case, for example, of a homily he gave in the week leading up to Pentecost 2016 in which he spoke of the Holy Spirit as the one who moves the Church and works in it. On this occasion, the Pope invited

---

its not always direct reception in the post-conciliar period, cf. W Kasper, *La Chiesa di Gesù Cristo. Scritti di ecclesiologia*, Queriniana, Brescia 2011, 231-234.

4 Cf. H de Lubac, *Paradosso e mistero della Chiesa*, Jaca Book, Milan 1997, 13-31. In English: *The Church: paradox and mystery*, Alba House (1969).

his congregation to call upon the Spirit in words that clearly express the Church's dependence on his action, which leads to Christ: 'Try to speak with him and to say: "I know that you are in my heart, that you are in the heart of the Church, that you create unity among us, all of us different, in all of our diversity,"'[5]

It is especially in his agenda-setting text, *Evangelii Gaudium* (*EG*) that we can grasp how the Church owes its being to God's presence and action. The way in which Francis says that the Church's centre is not the Church and that it is therefore de-centred in God's direction is a reminder that it owes its being to the gospel which is, etymologically speaking, the source of joy for all people.

Not very many commentators on this important magisterial text have spent time with its opening paragraphs, where the Pope has us understand that the Church only exists as a result of the gospel. In the very first sentences he says that 'The joy of the gospel fills the hearts and lives of all who encounter Jesus. Those who accept his offer of salvation are set free from sin, sorrow, inner emptiness and loneliness. With Christ joy is constantly born anew.'[6] What this gospel consists of is something Francis tells us a little further on, appealing to the words of his predecessor and making it clear that the gospel can be summed up in the encounter with the Person of Christ and thus with the love of God. The Pope says: 'I never tire of repeating those words of

---

5 Francis, *Morning meditation in the Domus Sanctae Marthae chapel*, Monday 9 May 2016.
6 *EG*, no. 1.

Benedict XVI which take us to the very heart of the Gospel: "Being a Christian is not the result of an ethical choice or a lofty idea, but the encounter with an event, a person, which gives life a new horizon and a decisive direction"[7] In the next paragraph of the same Apostolic Exhortation, the Pope clarifies how there can be no contradiction between christocentrism and theocentrism insofar as the encounter with the Person of Christ is *ipso facto* an encounter with the love of God himself.[8]

That the Church lives from this uninterrupted encounter with divine love is confirmed by what Francis says, again in this Exhortation, when describing the spirit of the evangelizer. In fact he shows that the claim of Christ's resurrection is not stating something about a past event but about the fact that he continues to be alive in the Spirit, in his victory over death and sin.[9] Encountering the Risen Lord means, for Christians, being placed under his loving gaze, which introduces us to God's love in a living relationship that lasts.[10]

---

7   A quotation from the Encyclical *Deus Caritas Est*, 2005: cf. AAS 98 (2006), p. 217. Cf. M GRONCHI, *Il sogno di papa Francesco*, cit., 18-19.

8   Cf. *EG*, no. 8.

9   Cf. *Ibidem*, nos 275-280, especially no. 276.

10   Cf. *Ibidem*, no. 264. Especially enlightening is what the Pope has to say about a Church which must allow itself always to be evangelized in order for it to evangelize. He says: "Consequently, we need to be constantly trained in hearing the word. The Church does not evangelize unless she constantly lets herself be evangelized. It is indispensable that the word of God 'be ever more fully at the heart of every ecclesial activity.' God's word, listened to and celebrated, above all in the Eucharist, nourishes and inwardly

2. *The gospel of mercy*

If there is any new emphasis in what Francis says about the primacy of God in the Church and which makes us think that we are grappling with a new stage in reception of the Council's magisterium, it is the central place that the 'gospel of mercy' has in his teaching.

For Francis, mercy is not just a secondary aspect of the gospel or something to be tackled equally with others. It has something fundamental to say about the face of God fully revealed in Christ. It is something that must already have been a beacon for the spirituality and ministry of Bergoglio the bishop, given that, in reference to Bede the Venerable, he chose as his episcopal motto *Miserando atque eligendo* ('While looking at me with eyes of mercy, he chose me').[11]

---

strengthens Christians, enabling them to offer an authentic witness to the Gospel in daily life. We have long since moved beyond that old contraposition between word and sacrament. The preaching of the word, living and effective, prepares for the reception of the sacrament, and in the sacrament that word attains its maximum efficacy" *Ibidem*, no. 174. Here we can appreciate a new and fruitful reception of what recent ecclesiology has now been highlighting for some time; the fact that the Church does not find its origins in some particular event in Jesus' life but in his entire mystery. It follows from this that Christ is not the *founder* relegated to the past but the perennial *foundation* alive and at work within the Church. On this view which has been shared for some time, cf. the summary offered by A ANTÓN, *El misterio de la Iglesia. Evolución histórica de las ideas eclesiológicas*, II, BAC, Madrid-Toledo 1986, 843-865, especially 861-862.

11 Cf. W KASPER, *Papa Francesco. La rivoluzione della tenerezza e dell'amore*, Queriniana, Brescia 2015, 49. (The work exists in English as *The Revolution of Tenderness and Love. Theological and Pastoral Perspectives*, Paulist Press; Translation edition, March

In any case, something central to the gospel is expressed by mercy, which can be summed up in Christ. Symptomatic of this are the opening words of *Misericordiae Vultus* (*MV*). 'Jesus Christ is the face of the Father's mercy. These words might well sum up the mystery of the Christian faith. Mercy has become living and visible in Jesus of Nazareth, reaching its culmination in him ... Whoever sees Jesus sees the Father (cf. Jn 14:9). Jesus of Nazareth, by his words, his actions, and his entire person reveals the mercy of God.'[12]

Here we are grappling with a fundamental aspect of the gospel that gives the Church its being and is a source of joy for humanity in contact with the most characteristic trait of God communicated in Christ. In the interview given to Tornielli, Francis says that, starting from the attitude and practice of Jesus as revealing God, it can be claimed that 'mercy is our God's identity card. God of mercy, God the merciful. For me this is really the identity card of our God.'[13] To come into contact with the Person of Christ who sums up the gospel, means to be related to the God who has a heart for the poor, especially those afflicted by the singular misery

---

6, 2015)) Cf. also FRANCIS, *Il nome di Dio è misericordia. Una conversazione con Andrea Tornielli*, Piemme, Milan 2016, 25-27 (Exists in English as *The Name of God is Mercy*, Random House; Translation edition, January 12, 2016).

12   *MV*, no. 1.

13   FRANCIS, *Il nome di Dio è misericordia*, cit., 24 (*The Name of God is Mercy*). Cf. W KASPER, *Misericordia, Concetto fondamentale del vangelo – chiave della vita cristiana*, Queriniana, Brescia 2015, 150-158 (In English as *Mercy. The Essence of the Gospel and the Key to Christian Life*, Paulist Press, April 16, 2014).

that is sin. All God's saving action, culminating in Jesus, can be summed up in this God who has heart for the miseries of humanity, including sin; and it has its foundation in the trinitarian being of God. 'With our eyes fixed on Jesus and his merciful gaze, we experience the love of the Most Holy Trinity. The mission Jesus received from the Father was that of revealing the mystery of divine love in its fullness. "God is love" (1 Jn 4:8,16), John affirms for the first and only time in all of Holy Scripture.'[14]

So what the Church lives for and exists from is this saving action of God where human misery is concerned, including sin, and which is seen supremely in Christ.[15] Mercy, as summarized by the parables in Lk 15, is, for the Pope, 'the core of the Gospel and of our faith, because mercy is presented as a force that overcomes everything, filling the heart with love and bringing consolation through pardon.'[16]

---

14 *MV*, no. 8. That such a perspective is plausible is confirmed by the extensive bibliography with which Kasper supports the fundamental importance of this category in Christ's message and life, as well as presenting it systematically: cf. W KASPER *Misericordia*, cit., 94-232. More recently, cf. G FERRETTI, *Il criterio midericordia. Sfide per la telogia e la prassi della Chiesa*, Queriniana, Brescia 2017. It could also be useful to see how mercy, clearly described in terms of divine transcendence, is also central in a classic author like Anselm, often misunderstood on this point. Cf. M CORBIN, *Introdction à l'*Epistola *et au* Cur Deus homo, in Anselme de Cantorbéry, *L'incarnation du Verbe. Pourquoi un Dieu-homme*, Cerf, Paris 1988, 15-163, 42-48.

15 This is said in probably the clearest way in FRANCIS, *Misericordia et Misera (MeM)*, nos 6-8 ,where the whole of liturgical life is interpreted as a realization of the divine mercy which gives the Church its being.

16 *MV*, no. 9.

It is what those who belong to the community of believers in Christ know they have experienced first.[17]

In this case too, it is clear that we are faced with a leap forward compared to what was said by Vatican II.

Reconsidering, in fact, the 'status' of Christian truth revealed by God, the last Council gave us the chance to highlight how we are dealing with a truth that involves human beings in their freedom and mutual relationship with God, though this latter is understood as being of an unequal nature. This is the turning point in *Dei Verbum* (*DV*), where Revelation is recognizable in the self-communication of God to human beings – whom he treats as friends (*DV*, 2) – also found in *Dignitatis Humanae* – which implicitly affirms that the religious freedom ascribed to members of other religious communities must also be presumed to exist for believers in Christ – leading to a clear rethinking of the 'status' of Christian truth.[18]

We now clearly see the overcoming of any presumed dichotomy between objectivity and subjectivity. When we consider, in fact, that God lets himself be encountered in Jesus and that this is what truth is, it is obvious we are dealing with a truth that involves us, and despite the unequalness of this relationship, people with their freedom,

---

17 Cf. FRANCIS, *Il nome di Dio è misericordia*, cit., 80.

18 A clear acknowledgement of this is seen in the third paragraph of *AG* 13, where it states that "The Church strictly forbids forcing anyone to embrace the Faith, or alluring or enticing people by worrisome wiles. By the same token, she also strongly insists on this right, that no one be frightened away from the Faith by unjust vexations on the part of others."

their individuality and their real situation are not at all unimportant.[19]

In Francis' teaching, this finds a new development by starting out from the consideration that the core of the gospel can be found in Divine Mercy, which appeared in definitive form in Christ. It follows from this that the gospel cannot be reduced to 'doctrine'; that God encounters human beings in the diversity of their cultures and takes hold of them in the individual circumstances of their life and situation; and that this encounter implies free assent on the part of the human being.

These are aspects that Francis clearly emphasizes when we are speaking of the Church in her act of evangelization but which, in some way, concern the Church also and primarily as addressed by the gospel and existing by virtue of it.

2.1 The gospel cannot be reduced to an idea

Given that the gospel consists of God's merciful love, it cannot be reduced to an 'abstract idea' or a 'doctrine'. This is not to say that there is no need for specific formulations of the faith in order to preserve the gospel. A superficial reading of some of Francis' expressions could lead to this conclusion. Rather are we dealing with the need to recognize that formulations of this kind are no excuse for obscuring the truth of the gospel of mercy.[20] These formulations have

19 On this cf. P CODA, *Il Concilio della Misericordia*, cit., 27-32.

20 To the interviewer who asked him if there was opposition

the task of preserving the gospel in its transcendence and making it available to every era and human being. So we need to consider how doctrinal formulas are the expression of the truth in its ongoing freshness, thus admitting that they are true in their finitude and in their being always necessarily the 'children' of a specific context. Therefore, they are always *definitive* and *temporary* at one and the same time, to use an expression adopted by Kasper some decades ago.[21] Such formulations cannot be, therefore, a prohibition of any effort to re-express the same truth in other ways so that the encounter between the living Christ in the Spirit and the people is truly realized. This is the perspective for locating and understanding what Pope Francis states in *EG*. The Pope says that given today's rapid cultural changes, we need to 'seek ways of expressing unchanging truths in a language which brings out their abiding newness,' to the point of saying that 'there are times when the faithful, in listening to completely orthodox language, take away something alien to the authentic Gospel of Jesus Christ, because that language is alien to their own way of speaking to and understanding one another. With the holy intent of communicating the

between truth and mercy or between doctrine and mercy, the Pope replied: "Mercy is true, the first attribute of God. So we can reflect theologically on doctrine and mercy, but without forgetting that mercy is doctrine. Nevertheless, I prefer to say: mercy is true" FRANCIS, *Il nome di Dio è misericordia*, cit., 75-76.

21 W KASPER, *Il dogma sotto la Paola di Dio*, Queriniana, Brescia 1968, 147-148. Cf. K RAHNER, *Che cos'è un asserto dogmatico?* In K RAHNER, *Saggi teologici, Paoline*, Rome 1965, 113-165, 121; and J RATZINGER, *Natura e compito della teologia. Il teologo nella disputa contemporanea. Storia e dogma*, Jaca Book, Milan 1993, 140.

truth about God and humanity, we sometimes give them a false god or a human ideal which is not really Christian.'[22] Without grasping the profound meaning and role of the doctrinal formulas, which do not prevent there being new formulations and, above all, new languages for expressing the faith, we could arrive at the paradoxical situation of listening to language which is formally orthodox but does not point us to the true gospel of Christ.[23] In this context, the same must also be said about the gospel which makes the Church what it is and by which the Church is constantly built up.

2.2 The gospel that needs to reach us

In the same way, it needs to be highlighted how the gospel builds up the Church and the Churches only if it reaches people within their various cultures and different life circumstances.

With regard to the former of these two aspects, what the Pope says about the language of the homily can be significant when he says that 'Christian preaching ... finds

22 *EG* no. 41.
23 Ratzinger has shown, in a very relevant way, how dogmatic formulations are of capital importance in that they allow us to express our common faith *together*. Of course, it does not follow from this that this is the only way the faith can be expressed. Regarding dogma, Ratzinger says something that is recognized by the best twentieth century theology and which bears fruit today in the promptings that come from Francis' magisterium: 'it is not the exclusive possibility of being able to say something only this way and not otherwise, but the possibility of being able to say it *in common* that is the foundation of its obligation and its permanence.' J Ratzinger, *Natura e compito della teologia*, cit., 138.

in the heart of people and their culture a source of living water, which helps the preacher to know what must be said and how to say it.'²⁴ With regard to the latter aspect, what he says in the now famous eighth chapter of *Amoris Laetitia* (*AL*) is especially instructive. It is clear there that there is an unequivocal gospel of the family as attested to in no. 292.²⁵ It is such, however, when it reaches families in their real life circumstances; and that is why constant discernment and accompaniment are essential, so that 'each person find his or her proper way of participating in the ecclesial community and thus to experience being touched by an "unmerited, unconditional and gratuitous" mercy. No one can be condemned for ever, because that is not the logic of the gospel! Here I am not speaking only of the divorced and remarried, but of everyone, in whatever situation they find themselves.'²⁶

---

24   *EG*, no. 139.

25   There it says that "Christian marriage, as a reflection of the union between Christ and his Church, is fully realized in the union between a man and a woman who give themselves to each other in a free, faithful and exclusive love, who belong to each other until death and are open to the transmission of life, and are consecrated by the sacrament, which grants them the grace to become a domestic church and a leaven of new life for society" *AL*, no. 292.

26   *Ibidem*, no. 297. To understand these aspects cf. S NOCETI, *Guida alla lettura della Esortazione Apostolica postsinodale di papa Francesco* Amoris Laetitia, in FRANCESCO, Amoris Laetitia. *La gioia dell'amore*, Piemme, Milan, 7-60, 45-50. C TORCIVIA, *Criteri per una lettura pastorale del capitolo ottavo di* Amoris Laetitia, Elledici, Leumann (TO) 2016, 18-24.

2.3 The gospel that calls for free adherence and conversion

The appeal to the gospel of mercy which builds up the Church cannot be misunderstood in any way as leading to indifference regarding the path of conversion asked of human beings or to the suggestion that sin is acceptable. Many who look with suspicion on Francis' insistence on the Divine Mercy, and many others who go in the opposite direction by referring to it with great emphasis have misunderstood him. In one or the other case they end up thinking of mercy as being so 'gratuitous' that it removes responsibility and therefore becomes inhuman.

A careful examination of the Pope's thinking, though, does not allow for any misunderstanding of the kind. Think of the appeal to the practice of *pilgrimage* in the Bull of Indiction for the Extraordinary Jubilee of Mercy, proposed as 'a sign that mercy is also a goal to reach and requires dedication and sacrifice. May pilgrimage be an impetus to conversion.'[27] But above all, think of the clear distinction he makes between *sinners and the corrupt*. While the former are constantly in need of the Divine Mercy and know that they need to look at themselves as being on the way, in a permanent state of conversion, the latter justify themselves and come to the point of not even having a sense of sin, like people with bad breath, the Pope says, turning once again to

---

27 *MV* no. 14. See also the strong invitation to conversion addressed to members of criminal organizations, to people who perpetrate or are involved in corruption, in no. 19 of the same document. The Pope speaks strongly to them telling them that "To stick to the way of evil will only leave one deluded and sad."

a fine metaphor, who are unaware of their state.[28]

> Corruption is the sin that instead of being recognized as such and making us humble, is elevated to a system, becomes a mental habit, a way of life. We no longer feel in need of mercy, but we justify ourselves and our behaviour. ... The repentant sinner, who then falls and falls because of his weakness, again finds forgiveness if he recognizes that he is in need of mercy. The corrupt, however, is the one who sins and does not repent, the one who sins and pretends to be a Christian, and gives scandal by his double life.[29]

Mercy, while being freely offered, is successful when it encounters people who, in their freedom, allow themselves to be touched by Christ and are converted. Thus, as Kasper

---

[28] FRANCIS, *Il nome di Dio è misericordia, (The Name of God is Mercy)* cit., 95. See the entire chapter. The examples he gives here as well as his clear denunciation of certain social sins and sins against creation which come from his more significant documents lead us to see how the category of sin and its dramatic nature has not disappeared. If there is something new to be noticed, then it is the fact that some social sins are very strongly denounced, compared to other sins the emphasis seems to have fallen on in the recent past.

[29] FRANCIS, *Il nome di Dio è misericordia (The Name of God is Mercy)*, cit., 92-93. We need to note how we are grappling with a distinction Jorge Bergoglio has been making since the 1990s and that he put to his diocese in Buenos Aires in December 2005. Cf. JM BERGOGLIO – FRANCIS, *Guarire dall corruzione*, Emi, Bologna 2013. In that context he showed, among other things, how there is a *qualitative leap* from the sinner to the corrupt person (pp. 34-35); and how one of the discriminating factors is that the corrupt person is closed off from transcendence (pp. 18-21).

has said, 'The discourse on God's mercy is not ... some nice rhetorical but harmless kind of talk. It does not wrap us up in the illusion of tranquillity and security: it gets us moving; it wants our hands and especially our hearts to be open.'[30]

It is not harmless talk for individual Christians and it is not for the Church either, which is the first great fruit of the Divine Mercy.

3. *The Church as mother. The importance of ecclesial mediation*

That the Church allow itself to be shaped and informed by the gospel of mercy which gives it its being, is of capital importance if it is to continue to still resonate within this world.

Here we have a fundamental aspect of the ecclesiology underlying Pope Francis's teaching: failure to grasp and explain it properly can lead to falsifying or not giving depth to many of his statements. This aspect could be summarized as follows: only a truly gospel-inspired Church can allow the gospel to continue on its way in the world; ecclesial mediation is essential for the merciful God who appeared in Christ to be able to reach humanity today. In other words, the question of God, which has become central in today's world, far from relativizing the question of the Church, makes it absolutely clear. In fact, only a Church which allows the God who appeared in Christ to shine through it can ensure that he remains alive and able to challenge humanity

---

30 W Kasper, *Papa Francesco. La rivoluzione della tenerezza e dell'amore (The Revolution of Tenderness and Love)*, cit., 55.

today and forever. He obviously transcends the Church, it is he who makes it exist; nevertheless, the gospel of mercy can continue to touch women and men only through the service of the Church.

Also in this case we are faced with a new phase of reception of the teaching of the Second Vatican Council, in particular of that dynamism of the mystery of the Church highlighted by the first chapter of *LG*, in which the light of Christ and the love of God allow themselves to be encountered only in the 'mirror' of the Church.[31]

This is the context for framing Francis' concern about the reform of the Church, a poor Church for the poor, a merciful Church.

In the address we have already quoted on the occasion of the 5th National Congress of the Italian Church, Francis once again spoke of an *ecclesia semper reformanda*. Confirming what we have just said, we need to recall that the reform Francis is speaking about is foreign to Pelagiansim, insofar as Church reform 'is not exhausted in the countless plans to

---

31 Cf. *Lumen Fidei* (*LF*), no. 37. The Pope says in this text: "The light of Christ shines, as in a mirror, upon the face of Christians; as it spreads, it comes down to us, so that we too can share in that vision and reflect that light to others, in the same way that, in the Easter liturgy, the light of the paschal candle lights countless other candles." For the importance this 'lunar' image of the Church's light had for the Fathers, cf. H RAHNER, *Simboli della Chiesa. L'ecclesiologia dei Padri*, San Paolo, Cinisello Balsamo (MI) 1995, 253-268: H DE LUBAC, *Paradosso e mistero della Chiesa*, cit., 15-18. For the way in which this theme flows into the Council, cf., V MARALDI, *Lo Spirito e la Sposa. Il ruolo ecclesiale dello Spirito Santo dal Vaticano I alla* Lumen Gentium *del Vaticano II*, Piemme, Casale Monferrato (AL) 1997, 279-296.

change her structures. It instead means being implanted and rooted in Christ, allowing herself to be led by the Spirit. Thus everything will be possible with genius and creativity.'[32] The Church must reform itself so that the *forma Christi* shines out in it; it is called to allow itself to be shaped by the Spirit in order to be conformed to its Lord; change of structures is relative to this being grafted onto Christ.

For this and only for this is it called to be *a Church which is poor and for the poor*. Only a poor Church, directed above all to the poor, the marginalized, the excluded, those discarded by society, can in fact become transparent of that Christ in which the whole gospel of God is condensed. The question of the poverty of the Church and her preference for the poor, far from being a mere sociological or economic question is, on the other hand, primarily a christological question and therefore a theological one. So In this sense, the words Francis used in *EG* regarding *a Church which is poor and for the poor* are unequivocal, especially in quoting the hymn from the Letter to the Philippians and appealing to the words of Benedict XVI:

> For the Church, the option for the poor is primarily a theological category rather than a cultural, sociological, political or philosophical one. God shows the poor 'his first mercy'. This divine preference has consequences for the faith life of all Christians, since we are called to have

---

32 FRANCIS, *Meeting with representatives at the 5th National Congress of the Italian Church* at the Cathedral of Santa Maria del Fiore, Florence, Tuesday, 10 November 2015.

> 'this mind... which was in Jesus Christ' (Phil 2:5). Inspired by this, the Church has made an option for the poor which is understood as a 'special form of primacy in the exercise of Christian charity, to which the whole tradition of the Church bears witness'. This option – as Benedict XVI has taught – 'is implicit in our Christian faith in a God who became poor for us, so as to enrich us with his poverty'. This is why I want a Church which is poor and for the poor.[33]

We need to recognize how we have a revival here, and a new hermeneutics, of what the Council already had highlighted in its fundamental paragraph 3 of *LG* 8, the last remnant of a much wider project of structuring the whole of the Council's discourse on the Church around the perspective of poverty.[34] This is a step – it needs to be recognized – often passed over in silence in the fifty or more years that now distance us from Vatican II. It is certainly not by chance that the theme would be repeated, with fresh emphasis, to the

33 *EG*, no. 198.
34 Cf. M Donati, *Il sogno di una Chiesa. Gli interventi al Concilio Vaticano II del cardinale Lercaro*, Cittadella, Assisi 2010, 197-227; G Ruggieri, *Evangelizzazione e stili ecclesiali*: Lumen Gentium *8,3*, in Associazione Teologica Italiana, *Annuncio del Vangelo*, forma Ecclesiae, San Paolo, Cinisello Balsamo (*MI*) 2005, 225-256. This concerns a theme which Congar came back to in a by now classic text: cf., YM Congar, *Per una chiesa serva e povera*, Qiqajon, Magnano (BI) 2014. The Italian edition also contains, on pp. 163-166, the famous "Pact of the Catacombs" signed by some bishops on 16 November 1965, shortly before the conclusion of the Council. Bergoglio has certainly known about this for a long time.

whole Church by a pope who comes from Latin America, and to a Church that has understood and developed it in recent decades: both at the level of theological reflection, and at the magisterial level.[35]

Something similar can be said, as we can work out from the quotation from *EG* 198 above, about the constant appeal Francis makes for a *merciful* Church, one that can look compassionately on the miseries of humanity to heal people's wounds, offer forgiveness and thus grant a new possibility of life. It is through a merciful Church that the gospel of mercy can, in fact, reach humanity today, be heard and experienced by women and men in flesh and blood and from within their circumstances of misery and sin.[36] What Francis said in the interview granted to Tornielli, mentioned previously, is an expression of this vision. The Pope says:

> Yes, I believe this is the time of mercy. The Church shows her maternal face, a mother's face, to wounded humanity. She does not wait

---

[35] In this regard we should recall Bergoglio's important role in drawing up the Aparecida Document, often quoted in *EG*. Galli maintains, regarding this, that "ayer Bergoglio contribuyó con Aparecida; hoy Aparecida contribuye con Francisco" (yesterday Bergoglio contributed to Aparecida; today Aparecida contributes to Francis). CM GALLI, *El "retorno" del Pueblo de Dios misonero*, cit., 439-440. Cf. also CM GALLI, *La Chiesa latino-americana e la teologia argentina con radici della* Evangelii gaudium, in FACOLTÀ TEOLOGICA DELL'ITALIA SETTENTRIONALE-SEZIONE DI TORINO (ed. R. Repole). *Siamo sempre discepoli-missionari* (Evangelii gaudium 120. *Quali "conversioni" per evangelizzare oggi?*, Dehoniane, Bologna (in the process of being published).

[36] Cf. *MeM*, nos 12-19.

for the wounded to knock at her door but goes out to find them on the road, gathers them up, embraces them, looks after the, makes them fell loved. ... This merciful love also illuminates the face of the Church and shows itself through the sacraments, especially reconciliation, and through communal and individual works of charity. Everything that the Church says and does manifests the mercy God has for man.[37]

The quotation is especially timely insofar as it contains an appeal to one of Francis' preferred metaphors for speaking about the Church: the Church as Mother.[38]

Considering his theological references, this should not be particularly surprising. Francis has expressly recognized a theological debt he has to his Jesuit confrere Henri de Lubac (especially for his work *Méditation sur l'Église*), for whom this image had considerable ecclesiological weight.[39] It is used by

---

37 FRANCIS, *Il nome di Dio è misericordia (The Name of God is Mercy)*, cit., 22-23. Cf. also the important pp. 76-83.

38 Galli often highlights this: cf. CM GALLI, *La teología pastoral de Aparecida, una de las raíces latinoamericanas de* Evangelii gaudium, cit. Cf. LF, nos 37-45; cf. M CRUCIANI, *Lo stile familiare di una evangelizzazione gioiosa*, in HM YAÑEZ (ed.), Evangelii gaudium: *il testo interroga. Chiavi di lettura, testimonianze e prospettive*, Gregorian & Biblical Press, Rome 2014, 95-108, 97-102.

39 It is Spadaro who makes note of how important it is for understanding Francis' ecclesiological vision of things to make reference to de Lubac's *Meditation on the Church*: A SPADARO, *La Biblioteca di papa Francesco* in *La Civiltà Cattolica* 165 (2014), 490-498. 496. In the interview granted the Editor of *La Civiltà Cattolica*, de Lubac is mentioned along with Certeau as one of the

the Pope to express precisely the function of mediation that the Church has, so that God's saving and merciful action will continue to reach humanity. Two presentations of catechesis held in St Peter's Square – September 3 and 10, 2014 – are particularly instructive in this regard for grasping its importance and function in Francis' thinking. The maternal image is useful for saying how it is by means of the Church that we are born to life in Christ through baptism; and it is only through this that we are reached by the gospel.[40] The Church, says the Pope, must therefore not be an NGO but must generate children, above all through the proclamation of the gospel. Since the gospel is about a God who has a heart for the miseries of humanity, this motherhood is also expressed in the merciful action of the Church: and here the Church, without taking anything away from the particular

---

two contemporary French thinkers the Pope prefers: cf. A Spadaro, *Intervista a papa Francesco* in *La Civiltà Cattolica* 164 (2013), 449-477, 450. ('Interview with Pope Francis' is available in English at http://w2.vatican.va/content/francesco/en/speeches/2013/september/documents/papafrancesco_20130921_intervista-spadaro.html). For the importance that the image takes on in de Lubac's ecclesiology, allow me to refer to R Repole, *Chiesa, pienezza dell'uomo. Oltre la postmodernità: G. Marcel e H. de Lubac*, Glossa, Milan 2002, 354-393. And for the difference in emphasis between de Lubac's and Pope Francis' use of it, cf. R Repole, *Introduzione alla Sezione terza chiesa*, in H de Lubac, *Le Chiese particolari nella Chiesa universale*, Jaca Book, Milan 2017, IX-XX, XX. The volume contains the text by de Lubac, *La maternità della Chiesa* in its second part.

40 Cf. Francis, *General audience, Wednesday 3 September 2014*. For the connection between the motherhood of the Church, its reform and its being a Church of mercy, cf. A Spadaro, *Intervista a papa Francesco*, cit., 461-464. Cf. note 39 above for English version.

role played by its ordained ministers, is to be understood as the totality of Christians.[41]

It is through the sacraments,[42] the proclamation of the gospel, the very existence of all Christians, their compassion and their bending over the wounds of humanity, that the gospel continues to be heard and alive in the world. It is therefore the motherhood of the Church that allows us to put the question of God back at the centre of things; not just 'any God', but the God who cares about and takes care of a miserable and sinful humanity.

Despite appearances to the contrary, the Pope believes we are dealing with a reality for which contemporary humanity has an infinite thirst.[43]

---

41 Cf. FRANCIS, *General audience, Wednesday 10 September 2014*. Cf. also what the Pope is expressing through the metaphor of the "Church as a field hospital": cf. A SPADARO, Intervista a papa *Francesco*, cit., 461-462. Cf. note 39 for English version.

42 Cf. *LF*, nos 40-45.

43 FRANCIS, *Il nome di Dio è misericordia (The Name of God is Mercy)*, cit., 30-31.

Chapter 2
THE 'HOLY FAITHFUL PEOPLE OF GOD'

1. *People of God: return to a central category*

If we ask ourselves who Francis is referring to when he speaks of the Church – which owes its being to the gospel of mercy and who is a mother allowing the merciful God to reach everyone – the answer appears to be clear: to the holy people of God. And due to this in particular, it is proper to say that we have entered a new phase of reception of Vatican II.

If an ecclesiological renewal could be expected on the eve of the Council, it was expected from a newfound centrality of the Pauline idea of the Church as the body of Christ.[1] But in fact, for a variety of reasons, the most important category

---

1 We are talking about texts like 1 Cor 12:4-29 and Rom 12:3-8, in which it is said that each member contributes to forming the body of Christ, and passages such as Eph 1:20-23; Col 1:15-20, in which the relationship between Christ the head, and the body is emphasized. The Pauline perspective is fruitful for a magisterial text of considerable importance for ecclesiological renewal, such as *Mystici Corporis* (1943) by Pius XII, as well as important ecclesiological studies. Among the latter, think, for example, of H DE LUBAC, *Méditation sur l'église*, Aubier-Montaigne, Paris 1952; and H DE LUBAC Corpus Mysticum. *L'eucharistie et l'église au moyen age*, Aubier-Montaigne 1949. To grasp the importance of the category on the eve of the last Council cf. YM CONGAR, *L'église de saint Augustin à l'époque moderne*, Cerf, Paris 2009, 413-472

with which Vatican II spoke of the Church was that of the people of God.[2] When, in *Lumen Gentium* (*LG*) there is a description of what the Church is as a mystery that becomes tangible in history, it is done by affirming above all that she is the people of God. The fact that the entire second chapter of the Constitution on the Church is dedicated to it and that Council texts refer to this category more than 184 times, are a clear indication of its centrality.[3]

The hermeneutics and post-conciliar reception, however, were not always peaceful and straightforward. With a view to curbing a sociological and democratizing interpretation of the people of God, the 1985 Synod of Bishops stated that the central and fundamental idea of the Council documents

---

2 Cf. D Vitali, *Popolo di Dio*, Cittadella, Assisi 2013, 119. Among significant studies for restoring the category in the pre-conciliar period, one cannot fail to mention MD Koster, *Ekklesiologie im Werden*, Bonifacius, Paderborn 1940. In the post-conciliar period, a text that expresses the effectiveness of this central category in *LG* well and concisely, and also the importance of not losing its reference to Christ in YM Congar, *Le concile de Vatican II. Son église peuple de Dieu et corps du Christ*, Beauchesne, Paris 1984, 109-122.

3 The importance of employing this category and the 'Copernican revolution' it is, given the position of this chapter, which precedes the one on the hierarchy (in particular the episcopate), have been brought out in a significant manner since the early post-Council years: cf. G Philips, *L'église et son mystère au deuxième Concile du Vatican. Histoire, texte et commentaire de la Constitution* Lumen gentium, tome I, Desclée, Paris 1966, 127-130; O Semmelroth *La Chiesa, nuovo popolo di Dio*, in G Baraúna, (ed.), *La Chiesa del Vaticano II. Studi e commenti intorno alla Costituzione dogmatica* Lumen gentium, Vallecchi, Florence 1965, 439-452.

was the ecclesiology of communion.[4] No doubt it was of assistance in guarding against likely misunderstandings in interpreting the category of 'people of God'; and it helped clarify that what lies at the foundation of the Church is communion with God. Therefore we can agree with what has been recently stated by Pottmeyer: 'There is one thing ... that is beyond discussion, that is, what Vatican Council II had most at heart: *communio* among members of the people of God can grow only to the extent that their *communio* with the trinitarian God grows.'[5]

One of the effects of this new stage of reception and interpretation of the Council was, however, that suspicion of this category lessened or, more to the point, it became a secondary issue, and as a consequence there was the risk that a view of Church became prominent in which the notion of communion could easily lead to either an excessive spiritualization or an excessively juridical approach.[6]

---

4 On this see R REPOLE, *Il Vaticano II e l'ecclesiologia di comunione,* in *Euntes docete* 65 (2012/3, 39-53). Kasper, an authoritative commentator on the Synod, has clearly explained how one of the risks that it intended to respond to had been a unilateral interpretation of the concept of the people of God: cf. W KASPER, *Teologia e Chiesa,* Queriniana, Brescia 1989, 298-300.

5 HJ POTTMEYER, *La Chiesa in cammino, per configurarsi come popolo di Dio,* in A SPADARO – CM GALLI (eds.), *La Riforma e le riforme nella Chiesa,* Queriniana, Brescia 2016, 66-81, 81.

6 Cf. G LAFONT, *Immaginare la Chiesa cattolica. Linee e approfondimenti per un nuovo dire e un nuovo fare della comunità cristiana,* San Paolo, Cinisello Balsamo (MI) 1998, 96; and J RIGAL, *L'ecclésiologie de communion. Son volution historique et ses fondements,* Cerf, Paris 1997, 241.

What is very clear, as we look at Pope Francis' magisterium, is that we are seeing a rediscovered central role for the category of the people of God.

From the outset of his papacy he has made this unequivocally clear.

> The image of the church I like is that of the holy, faithful people of God. This is the definition I often use, and then there is that image from the Second Vatican Council's 'Dogmatic Constitution on the Church'(No. 12). Belonging to a people has a strong theological value. In the history of salvation, God has saved a people. There is no full identity without belonging to a people. No one is saved alone, as an isolated individual, but God attracts us looking at the complex web of relationships that take place in the human community. God enters into this dynamic, this participation in the web of human relationships. The people itself constitutes a subject. And the church is the people of God on the journey through history, with joys and sorrows. Thinking with the church, therefore, is my way of being a part of this people.[7]

The first part of Chapter 2 of *Evangelii Gaudium* (*EG*) is valuable confirmation of the central role played, in Francis' thinking, of a category that is so deeply rooted in Scripture,

---

7   A Spadaro, *Interview with Pope Francis*, http://w2.vatican.va/content/francesco/en/speeches/2013/september/documents/papa-francesco_20130921_intervista-spadaro.html

tradition and liturgical prayer. The above quotation, and a reading of *EG* allow us to discern how this rediscovered centrality enables the Pope to once again highlight in a new and relevant way some important aspects of the ecclesiology put forward by the Council and then developed in theology following it. Reading Pope Francis' words also lets us glimpse his own particular theological interpretation of the Church as the people of God.

1.1 God chooses and saves a people

Among the aspects given renewed emphasis in Francis' teaching, we need to mention especially the fact that the Church manifests God's intention to save human beings not individually but in their belonging to his people. Hence it becomes obvious that being saved means moving away from self-centredness and individualism and being open to God and our brothers and sisters. Chapter Two of *LG* (no. 9) says: 'Rather has it pleased Him to bring men together as one people, a people which acknowledges Him in truth and serves Him in holiness.' The reference here is to the people of Israel who are further described in the same paragraph, in the light of what Jesus brought them, as the 'messianic people.' The Pope gives clear evidence of this feature of a Church seen as the people of God, meaning that God chooses us in choosing his people and saves us within the context of the relationships we experience as part of this people: we gather this from the quotation given above and from what he says, just as explicitly, in *EG*. Here the Pope says that God, in offering salvation, has called human beings together 'as a people and not as isolated individuals. No one is saved by himself or herself, individually, or by his or her own efforts. God attracts us by taking into account the complex interweaving of personal relationships entailed in the life of a human community.'[8]

This dimension of Church has an especially prophetic resonance in our contemporary Western world in which one of the effects of postmodernity is represented by the dehumanizing outcomes of libertarian individualism where individuals feel they are not bound by anything and are the subjects of endless rights.[9] In the scheme of Pope Francis' thinking, this observation is quite heartfelt: just consider how, in *Laudato Si'* (*LS*), he connects human beings' indifference to nature and the earth with their indifference to one another, especially the weakest;[10] and as another example, think how in EG he identifies one of the temptations that can even effect pastoral workers (laity or priests) when they become selfish with free time.[11]

1.2 The universal scope of the Church

Considering the Church as the people of God allows him to give more visibility to its universal scope. One of Francis' real concerns, justifying the invitation in this agenda-setting text to 'a new phase of evangelization, one

---

8 *EG*, no. 113. We see that in a footnote he refers to the succinct statement in *Lumen Gentium* 9.

9 Cf. L BRUNI – S ZAMAGNI, *L'economia civile*, Il Mulino, Bologna 2015, 130-136.

10 Cf. *LS*, nos 115-121.

11 Cf. *EG*, nos 81-83.

marked by enthusiasm and vitality,'[12] is for the Church to remain open to everyone so that whoever is part of it feels called and so that each person can feel at home in it. The Council appealed to this too, stating that all of humanity is called to the people of God, which is the universal sacrament of salvation.[13] Speaking directly, and in language steeped in hope, the Pope launches this idea in new terms: 'To those who feel far from God and the Church, to all those who are fearful or indifferent, I would like to say this: the Lord, with great respect and love, is also calling you to be a part of his people!'[14] It could be enlightening to note how this universality is once again connected with the idea of a merciful Church where everyone can find hospitality. In the next paragraph in *EG* he says: 'The Church must be a place of mercy freely given, where everyone can feel welcomed, loved, forgiven and encouraged to live the good life of the Gospel.'[15] Indeed, there is an intrinsic connection between this universality and mercy – in God first and then in the Church as a consequence – which allows those who are furthest away, the poor, sinners, to be brought to the

---

12 *Ibidem*, no. 17.

13 A summary of the Council's position on this can be found in G CANOBBIO, *Chiesa perché. Salvezza dell'umanità e mediazione ecclesiale,* San Paolo, Cinisello Balsamo (MI) 1994, 131-156.

14 *EG*, no. 113. We can find the same thought clearly expressed in the interview granted Spadaro: "This church with which we should be thinking is the home of all, not a small chapel that can hold only a small group of selected people. We must not reduce the bosom of the universal church to a nest protecting our mediocrity." A SPADARO, *Interview with Pope Francis*, cit.

15 *EG*, no. 115.

fore: only when they are reached out to can there be true universality, which should never start out from those who are 'closest'. In this regard too we cannot fail to note the new emphasis with which Francis relaunches this universal scope of the Church. He is the first pope to come from Latin America, and with him the world's peripheries are now located at the Church's centre,[16] allowing them to better grasp how its universality can only but bring the poor and those most in need of mercy to the fore. Latin America is the 'most unequal subcontinent; it is marked by inequality,' says the Argentinian theologian Galli, 'which challenges the Christian conscience. Poverty and Christianity overlap in it: many live in poverty, starting from their faith and we all have to live our faith to overcome unjust poverty. The option for the poor and Catholic popular religiosity are the characteristics of a Church of the poor.'[17]

1.3 Equal dignity and shared responsibility of all Christians

The unequivocally most important aspect given us by an ecclesiology of the people of God, however, is that of

16 Cf. CM GALLI, *La riforma missionaria della Chiesa secondo Francesco. L'ecclesiologia del popolo di Dio evangelizzatore*, in A SPADARO – CM GALLI (eds.), *La Riforma e le riforme nella Chiesa*, cit., 37-65, 37-38.

17 CM GALLI, *Il forte vento del Sud*, in *Il Regno/At.* 59 (2014/2), 57-63, 59. The option for the poor has been interpreted by other important expressions of Latin American theology as well as being the feature that enables genuine universality: see for example J SOBRINO, *Gesù Cristo liberatore. Lettura storico-teologica di Gesù di Nazareth*, Cittadella, Assisi 1995, 63-67. This work is available in English as *Jesus the Liberator* Orbis Books (March 1, 1994).

the equal dignity and shared responsibility of all Christians. It is something that emerges strongly and decisively in *EG* when the Pope recognizes that the evangelizer is not just some individual but the whole people of God, all Christians.[18] We find this in any of his addresses where, in various ways, he distances himself from any kind of clericalism. Particularly instructive regarding the renewed way in which this perspective of the Council is relaunched for the Church today by Francis is what he says in the letter sent to the President of the Pontifical Commission for Latin America and the Caribbean, Cardinal Ouellet. One could object here to the use of the term 'lay' in speaking of the Christian as such. Moreover, the question of whether or not we should maintain a theology of the laity or whether this is somehow superseded by a theology of the people of God is something that has been much debated in the post-Council period. There are still varying theological positions on this.[19] However, the decisiveness and freshness with which Francis proposes the teaching that being Christian is the most profound identity of all believers in Christ, cannot be debated. Francis says:

18   Cf. *EG*, 120-121.
19   A recent text like P NEUNER, *Per una teologia del popolo di Dio,* Queriniana, Brescia 2016, seems somehow to 'dissolve' the category of the lay Christian in the re-found centrality of the people of God. In my opinion, more convincingly, Canobbio tries to preserve its plausibility as a 'symbolic figure' of something that concerns the whole Church. See the volume (also useful for reconstructing the entire pre- and post-Council debate on this): G CANOBBIO, *Laici o cristiani? Elementi storico-sistematici per una descrizione del cristiano laico,* Morcelliana, Brescia 1997.

> ... we all make our entry into the Church as lay people. The first sacrament, the one that forever seals our identity, and of which we should always be proud, is baptism. Through it and through the anointing of the Holy Spirit, (the faithful) "are consecrated as a spiritual house and a holy priesthood" (*LG*, no. 10, *EV* 1/311). Our first and fundamental consecration has its roots in our baptism. ... It is good to remember that the Church is not an elite of priests, consecrated persons, bishops, but that we all form the holy faithful people of God. ... We are, as Vatican Council II points out very well, the people of God whose identity is "the dignity and freedom of the sons of God, in whose hearts the Holy Spirit dwells as in His temple" (*LG* no. 9; *EV* 1/309).[20]

In the context, therefore, of this perspective of the people of God, Francis means by 'Church' the totality and communion of the baptized, whose dignity comes from being children in the Son by virtue of the anointing of the Spirit who dwells in each of them. This clearly does not detract from or diminish the significance and importance of ordained ministers within God's people, but it makes their ministerial function clear: they are within the Church, at the service of its existence. Their *raison d'être* is not, therefore, to be sought 'in themselves and for themselves',

---

20 FRANCIS, *Il santo popolo fedele di Dio,* in *Il Regno / Doc* 61 (2106/7), 201-204, 202.

but in their pastoral service to the people of whom they are a part and who call on them to be in close contact with other Christians. Francis, once again, and in the same document, says: 'A pastor cannot be thought of without a flock which he is called to serve. The pastor is a shepherd of a people, and the people make use of him from within. Very often we go ahead, paving the way, at other times we retrace our steps to see that no one is left behind, and quite often we are in their midst, gauging the pulse of the people.'[21]

1.4 Popular, not populist. The challenge of a mystical fraternity

To grasp the clear direction the Pope has given to this ecclesiological vision and to show how the category of people of God does not have to end up with the misunderstandings the 1985 Synod of bishops was reacting to, Francis' concern to distinguish this vision of the people of God from any kind of populism is quite indicative.

In this case, this means unequivocally distancing oneself from considering the people of God as an ecclesial subject to the detriment of or, worse, in opposition to others. Francis says that by people of God he means 'pastors and people together. The Church is the totality of God's people.'[22] He seems to be also distancing himself from a populist interpretation when relaunching the Council's teaching on the universal call to holiness in the Church. He says he appreciates and invites us to recognize the 'daily holiness'

21 *Ibidem*, no. 201.
22 A SPADARO, *Interview with Pope Francis*, cit.

of this people, something that can be recognized in every member of the Church in whatever situation in life. This holiness is associated with patience: not only as taking charge of the events and circumstances of life but also as constancy in going forward, day by day.[23] We find a similar distancing from the risk of populism in the repeated invitation to think not just of qualified workers but of each and every one of the baptized as being active members of the people of God.[24]

What could be said is that Francis infers a 'popular' notion of Church from his vision of Church as the people of God. This means that it is essential to involve the voice and contribution of everyone and that no group – clerical or lay – can claim to be everyone or to replace others.

Seen positively, this perspective translates into a vision of a people of God which is such by virtue of the fraternal bonds that exist between Christians, something that is a given and at the same time sought after through the power of the Holy Spirit. Precisely for this reason it is a fraternity that calls on the freely chosen involvement of every individual.[25] At the same time, it is a fraternity that is possible only on the basis of regarding the other person in a way that implies openness to God's otherness and to God as we see him in our brother or sister. The Pope sums this up vividly in *EG* 92, where he finds the true medicine for the disease of individualism in what he says is a mystical fraternity. Francis says that it is the choice of fraternity which is true healing,

23   Cf. *Ibidem*, cit.
24   *EG*, no. 120.
25   Cf. *Ibidem*, no. 91.

> ... since the way to relate to others which truly heals instead of debilitating us, is a mystical fraternity, a contemplative fraternity. It is a fraternal love capable of seeing the sacred grandeur of our neighbour, of finding God in every human being, of tolerating the nuisances of life in common by clinging to the love of God, of opening the heart to divine love and seeking the happiness of others just as their heavenly Father does.[26]

The above passage is very suitable for showing how Francis' concept of the Church as God's people overcomes the danger of an exclusively sociological interpretation of the category. There is no interpersonal bond with our brothers and sisters which is not, in fact, rooted in God; just as there is no bond with God that does not involve the gift of self, openness and ' ... reconciliation with others.'[27]

The people of God is possible on the basis of this distinct yet unique love, because of the reality of Christ, *the Word of God made flesh*: love of God and love of neighbour. The interpersonal communion among believers that is brought about, in Christ, by virtue of the presence and action of the Spirit, is the sign in this world of the vocation to communion with God and our brothers and sisters to which every human being is called.

---

26 *Ibidem*, no. 92.
27 *Ibidem*, no. 88.

2. 'Circumdata varietate' *and 'the coat of many colours'*

For some of the Fathers of the Church or medieval writers, the long robe of the Patriarch Joseph (Gen 37) is seen as being made of many colours, and because of this, adopted as a symbol of the Church which is one but resplendent for the variety of its peoples and cultures.[28]

One of the undoubted advantages of using the category of the people of God in speaking of the Church is also that we can better highlight its *catholicity*. In fact, God's people are immersed in history: from this and from the fact of their universality, it follows that God's people cannot be thought of as being on the margins of all the different peoples who inhabit the earth, and of all their cultures.

Insofar as it is *God's* people we are talking about, hence the result of divine initiative and the gospel, the Church clearly cannot be fully described just as people and their cultures, but, nonetheless, nor can it exist unless it is inculturated within them.

In this case too we are grappling with an aspect that was made clear by the last Council. We see this just by looking at its intentions and effects. Vatican II was the expression of a Church that wanted to finally enter into dialogue with modern culture, by contrast with the abysmal distance between them that had existed for centuries. The consequence was an improved perception of the Church, though just beginning to be so, as not just a European Church, but one inhabited by the many peoples of the earth.

28 Cf. H DE LUBAC, *Cattolicismo. Aspetti sociali del dogma*, Jaca Book, Milan 1992, 222.

We see this awareness even when we look at the Council's texts. We understand through them, however, that this is a 'task' that lies ahead and that fidelity to the Council must pass through a Church capable of being inculturated in the gospel and of then inculturating this gospel it lives by in the many peoples and their cultures. Just by way of example, think of a text like *LG* 13 which says that the people of God 'takes nothing away from the temporal welfare of any people. On the contrary it fosters and takes to itself, insofar as they are good, the ability, riches and customs in which the genius of each people expresses itself. Taking them to itself it purifies, strengthens, elevates and ennobles them'; and if we also consider the relationship between Church and culture as conceived by *Gaudium et Spes* (*GS* nos 53-62).

2.1 Reference to the 'theology of the people'

Without doubt, this 'task', following the Council, was taken up generously and creatively by the Latin American Churches and in a special way by the Argentinian Church. This also gave birth to the theological renewal that took place through the so-called theology of liberation and its typically Argentinian version of this theology called the 'theology of the people'.[29] The latter's principal exponent in

---

29   To understand its peculiarity and to reconstruct its history, cf. M Castagnaro, *La teologia di Francesco. Intervista a Juan Carlos Scannone*, in *Il Regno / At* 58 (2013/6), 128; JC Scannone, *La teologia argentina del pueblo*, in *Gregorianum* 96 (2015/1), 9-24; JC Scannone, *Perspectivas eclesiologicas de la «teología del pueblo» en la Argentina*, in F Chica – S Panizzolo – H Wagner (eds), *Ecclesia tertii millennii advenientis. Omaggio al P. Angel Antón*, Piemme,

the era immediately following the Council was the Italo-Argentinian theologian Lucio Gera, who provided one of the first commentaries on the first chapter of *LG*.[30] The theology of the people has also seen a degree of development in recent decades.

It is characterized by the fact that it looks at the people in the light of its unity, and interprets social injustice therefore as anti-people. 'People' is not seen in dialectical terms as a class which is oppressed by the capitalist system. Rather is it seen from a socio-cultural perspective as the subject of a common history and culture; and it is seen as the bearer of its own culture, understood as 'the common lifestyle of a people.'[31] Culture, therefore, takes on a sociological and ethnic significance, following the view which already characterized the reception of *GS* 53 at Puebla.[32]

Casale Monferrato (*AL*) 1997, 686-704, 690-691.

30   Cf. L GERA, *El misterio de la Iglesia*, in VR AZCUY – JC CAAMAÑO – CM GALLI (eds), *La Eclesiología del Concilio Vaticano II*, cit., 97-171. In this text, he saw and already lucidly recalled how 'el misterio se manifestia también en la historia de la Iglesia' (p. 108).

31   Cf. JC SCANNONE, *La teología argentina del pueblo*, cit., 12-13.

32   In the Puebla Document, for which Lucio Gera was one of those responsible, no. 386 says: "Con la palabra «cultura» se indica el modo particular como, en un pueblo, los hombres cultivan su relación con la naturaleza, entre sí mismos y con Dios (GS 53b) de modo que puedan llegar a «un nivel verdadero y plenamente humano» (GS 53a). Es «el estilo de vida común» (GS 53c) que caracteriza a los diversos pueblos; por ello se habla de «pluralidad de culturas» (GS 53c)." Scannone notes that the expression "en un pueblo" does not appear in *GS* 53 and is affected by the typically Argentinian reception of the text: "así se desplaza el sentido conciliar

From this theological perspective the people of God can only exist in a structural way among the many peoples, meaning in different cultures: it is the one people of God but existing concretely as inhabited by the plurality of peoples and cultures in which it lives.

2.2 The people in the peoples

It is evident that this theology became part of Francis' ecclesiology and shows through, today, in his documents, especially *EG*; this is how a new phase in the reception of the Council's ecclesiology has been set in motion and is now taking place, also as the result of a specific theological development offered by South American theology and especially Argentinian theology. In the light of what we have pointed out, it is understandable why nos 115-118 of *EG* are subtitled 'A people of many faces' and why the Pope is passing on a vision of the people of God which is embodied in different peoples and enriched by their culture without at the same time being confused or being fully identified with any of them.

---

más humanista de cultura de ambos primeros párrafos, hacía el que el Concilio relaciona luego su 'aspecto histórico y social' y denomia 'sentido sociólogico y etnológico' que la Consitución aborda sólo en el tercer párrafo (53c). Por consequiente, Puebla relee 53 a y b desde la óptica de 53 c y, por ello, cambia el ángulo de enfoque de su comprensión de la cultura." *Ibidem*, 12-13. Scannone notes how this interpretation came about spontaneously: cf. JC Scannone, *Incarnazione, kénosis, inculturazione e povertà*, in A Spadaro – CM Galli, (eds), *La Riforma e le riforme nella Chiesa*, cit., 459-484, 463-464.

> The People of God is incarnate in the peoples of the earth, each of which has its own culture. The concept of culture is valuable for grasping the various expressions of the Christian life present in God's people. It has to do with the lifestyle of a given society, the specific way in which its members relate to one another, to other creatures and to God. Understood in this way, culture embraces the totality of a people's life.[33]

Still within the context of such a theological approach, we can understand, then, what Francis says, echoing the *gratia paesupponit naturam* of Thomas,[34]: 'Grace supposes culture, and God's gift becomes flesh in the culture of those who receive it.'[35] People do not only exist as individuals, detached from relationships with other people; they exist in a specific people and therefore share in a common lifestyle. As a consequence, evangelization is to *become part* of and *transfigure* cultures.

By inhabiting the different cultures and being 'incarnated' in the different peoples who come to form the one people of God, the Church finds itself enriched, and is in some way indebted to them in order to be what it is; at the same time the Church discovers new aspects of revelation. In words that

---

33 *EG*, no. 115.

34 Cf. *Summa Theologiae, I,2,2*, ad 1: "Sic enim fides praesupponit cognitionem naturalem, sicut gratia naturam, et ut perfectio perfectibile".

35 *EG*, no. 115. On this aspect, cf. D Albarello, *La grazia suppone la cultura. Ordine culturale e pensiero della fede alla luce di* Evangelii gaudium, in *Teologia* 41 (2106/2), 222-248.

on the one hand express traditional features of the notion of the Church's catholicity and on the other are tinged with the contribution typical of Argentinian theology, the Pope says that 'In the Christian customs of an evangelized people, the Holy Spirit adorns the Church, showing her new aspects of revelation and giving her a new face.'[36]

This vision of a people of God living in different peoples implies, however, that there is no culture within which one can consider the Church to be fully identified. To do so would mean making the gospel unavailable for other cultures and preventing Christ, alive in the Spirit, from encountering and being encountered by other people who are always 'culturally situated'. This would ultimately compromise the catholicity of the Church. Francis therefore warns of the duty to be clear that:

> While it is true that some cultures have been closely associated with the preaching of the Gospel and the development of Christian thought, the revealed message is not identified with any of them; its content is transcultural. Hence in the evangelization of new cultures, or cultures which have not received the Christian message, it is not essential to impose a specific cultural form, no matter how beautiful or ancient it may be, together with the Gospel. The message that we proclaim always has a certain cultural dress, but we in the Church can sometimes fall into a needless hallowing of our

---

36 *EG*, no. 116.

own culture, and thus show more fanaticism than true evangelizing zeal.[37]

The quotation shows how such an ecclesiological perspective is in fact critical of a universalist vision of the Church where unity does not imply real plurality and which inevitably ends up sacrilizing a single culture and extending it to all peoples. It seems likewise clear that such a theology of Church involves and calls for a structural reform (which we will discuss later) which foresees the real overcoming of centralism and as a result fosters effective decentralization. Indeed, we cannot conceive of a Church as the people of God existing in different peoples if there are no ecclesial structures that allow and make it truly possible.

On the other hand, what Francis says is also a a symptom of how complex the problem of the relationship between the gospel and culture really is. It is also true that the gospel transcends every culture and, if this is so, it must be able to express itself and be heard in every era and in all the cultures of humanity. There has never been nor will there ever be a gospel in its 'pure state' and which is not already really part of one or other culture. Even those who dream of a return to Scripture will have to recognize that the gospel always reaches us from within certain cultures there that are, for the most part, far from the culture we experience today.

3. Sensus fidei. *A new and provocative interpretation*

The perspective of an ecclesiology revolving around the category of God's people, with all this means for

37 *Ibidem*, no. 117.

shedding light on equal dignity, true *aequalitas* (*LG*, 32) and the common responsibility of all Christians, enabled the Council Fathers to recover the doctrine of the *sensus fidelium*. *LG* 12 is a crucial passage for understanding how there is an infallibility *in credendo* on which infallibility *in docendo* is based.

However, we need to see that other than a few mentions here and there, this is a theme that has not so often appeared in the post-conciliar magisterium.[38] It would therefore seem to be a valuable novelty – which once again leads us to say that Francis's magisterium regarding ecclesiology is bringing the Church into a new phase of reception of Vatican II. In *EG*, Francis takes this theme up broadly. He says:

> In all the baptized, from first to last, the sanctifying power of the Spirit is at work, impelling us to evangelization. The people of God is holy thanks to this anointing, which makes it infallible *in credendo*. This means that it does not err in faith, even though it may not find words to explain that faith. The Spirit guides it in truth and leads it to salvation. As part of his mysterious love for humanity, God furnishes the totality of the faithful with an instinct of faith – *sensus fidei* – which helps them to discern what is truly of God. The presence of the Spirit gives Christians a certain connaturality with divine

---

38 Cf. D VITALI, *Una Chiesa di popolo: il sensus fidei come principio dell'evangelizzazione*, in HM YAÑEZ (ed.), *Evangelii gaudium: il testo interroga*, cit., 53-66, 58-59.

realities, and a wisdom which enables them to grasp those realities intuitively, even when they lack the wherewithal to give them precise expression.[39]

Here, Francis is recalling and now relaunching a Council doctrine that has been central throughout his previous ministry.[40] So the emphases he puts on it are connected with his own experience and developments in this issue in the Latin American Church and the theology developed there.

3.1 The meaning of divine things and the possibility of expressing them

The Pope recalls how, by virtue of the anointing of the Holy Spirit, all Christians are granted a connaturality with divine realities and a capacity to discern what comes from God, so that God's people may be guided to the truth. We can see here an aspect of Francis' ecclesiology that already emerges from what was said above and that it is now appropriate to point out that the people of God is not something static; rather is it a dynamic reality insofar as it is a messianic, pneumatic people and, therefore, a subject inhabited by the Spirit and guided by him to the 'whole truth.'[41] Seen this way, we can grasp the full meaning of

---

39 *EG*, no. 119. A note refers to the text of *LG* 12. Cf. also A SPADARO, *Interview with Pope Francis*, cit.

40 Galli says that "since 1974 Bergoglio has been expounding the Council's teaching on the *sensus fidei fidelium and infallibility in credendo of the holy People* (*LG* 12)." CM GALLI, *El "retorno" del Pueblo de Dios misionero*, cit., 454.

41 If we think of ecclesiological development following the

the reference to the *sensus fidei* as a sense that allows us to discern what comes from God, within a journey toward the whole truth.

The way in which Francis relaunches the importance of this ecclesiological doctrine recovered from the Council also displays a clearly new emphasis that most likely comes from his long pastoral experience, carried out within a Church such as the Argentinian Church. We refer to the attention he gives to the fact that the people of God has the ability to grasp, live and transmit the faith even when it lacks the conceptual tools for doing so. This is an emphasis of significant importance as it allows us, first of all, to recognize how the act of faith is even more profound than its formulation: the formulation is rooted in the former.[42] This is an invitation to those in the Church who have the task of correctly expressing and transmitting the faith, to remain rooted in the faith which is believed, lived and celebrated by the people of God.

This new emphasis can likewise be useful for recognizing how, in the variety which is the people of God, there can be different approaches to and 'languages' for expressing the faith.

Council, we see that this is a feature which is especially evident in a significant text like that of YM CONGAR, *Un popolo messianico. The chiesa sacramento di salvezza. La salvezza e la liberazione*, Queriniana, Brescia 1976.

42 This is what implicitly underlies Aquinas' famous expression, that the act of the believer "non terminatur ad enuntiabile, sed ad rem": *Summa Theologiae*, II-II, 1. 1, a.2 ad 2.

3.2 Popular piety, its value and limitations

The typical contribution of the theology of the people in the way Francis interprets and once again proposes the doctrine of the sensus *fidei fidelium* can be found in the fact that he relates it to the question of popular piety.

Far from despising it, Argentinian theology has interpreted popular piety as an expression of the *sensus fidei fidelium* and has seen popular piety as part of a virtuous circle including the ecclesiological category of the people of God: in fact, the latter is recognized in the great manifestations of popular piety while popular piety is purified and transformed by the reality of the people of God.[43] In *EG* we can see how Francis connects the *sensus fidei* to popular piety, given the way he talks about it. In fact, the Pope presents popular piety as an expression of the inculturated gospel and invites us to read its actions as expressions of theological life, since the Holy Spirit with which Christians are anointed, is at work there. As Francis puts it: 'no one who loves God's holy people will view these actions as the expression of a purely human search for the divine. They are the manifestation of a theological life nourished by the working of the Holy Spirit who has been poured into our hearts (cf. Rom 5:5).'[44] Precisely because of this indwelling of the Spirit in the hearts of Christians, Francis sees popular

---

43 Cf. JC SCANNONE, *Perspectivas eclesiologicas de la «teología del pueblo» en la Argentina*, cit., 696-697; CM GALLI, *El "retorno" del Pueblo de Dios misionero*, cit., 452-454; CM GALLI, *La riforma missionaria della Chiesa secondo Francesco*, cit., 52.

44 *EG*, no. 125.

piety as 'a spirituality incarnated in the culture of the lowly.'[45] This is a quotation from the Aparecida Document to which Bergoglio's contribution was fundamental, and it is now used by the Pope to affirm how faith expresses itself in popular piety, though more by way of symbols than by discursive reasoning, as he says, and despite the emphasis falling more on the *credere in Deum* than the *credere Deum* of the act of faith. In popular piety, it is more the personal, filial abandon with which believers, especially the poorest,[46] give themselves to God, than any believing knowledge of God and his plan of salvation.[47] As an expression of the Christian faith and genuine theological life, the actions of popular piety are even to be seen as a locus theologicus to give particular attention to when we are looking to the new evangelization.[48]

It seems pretty much clear that the perspective laid down by Francis in this regard is strongly influenced by the theology of the people and the direction taken by the Latin American Church in recent decades (not least the direction that came to maturity with Aparecida) and the ecclesial situation in that context. Given the specific nature of the question, critical reflection is required, especially given that

45 *Ibidem*, no. 124.
46 *Cf. Ibidem*, no. 125
47 To make this distinction clearer, we can recall what Francis says elsewhere: "This is how it is with Mary: If you want to know who she is, you ask theologians; if you want to know how to love her, you have to ask the people." A SPADARO, *Interview with Pope Francis*, cit.
48 Cf. *EG*, no. 126.

we need to reconcile such a development in the Council's teaching in the context of Churches within cultures that are very different from one another.

In the first instance, we might well accept the invitation to look at the reality of the Church now coming from the so-called south of the world in which most Christians live, and for many of whom popular piety can really be the most normal and natural way of expressing and living their Christian and ecclesial spirituality. Some suspicions about this, found in secularized Europe, may be the legacy of a Church and a theology which is still strongly Eurocentric.

Then we need to consider, in this discussion, how we prioritize listening to this faith of Christians including when they do not have the appropriate categories and theological tools. The question is of the utmost importance and can also be extended to other Church issues such as the shared responsibility of all believers. There may be the danger of confusing real listening with listening to just some Christians only: the more acculturated or more 'clericalized' ones. Similarly, the shared responsibility of all Christians can be confused with the sharing in ecclesial life of those who have adopted a specific kind of language. Here, we cannot fail to note how Francis also sees popular piety as an expression of the evangelizing activity of everyone, beginning with the simplest and poorest.[49] It is one of the ways in which the poor are not only recipients of the Church's attention, but

---

49 Cf. *Ibidem*, no. 126. On the active role of the poor, cf. JC SCANNONE, *Incarnazione, kénosos, inculturazione e povertà*, cit., 475-477.

are key players in its mission. The discourse could, however, be broadened to ask whether it might be just as urgent to grasp the *sensus fidei* of Christians living and expressing their faith in other contexts, thus having confidence in other languages: for example, the languages of the various sciences in which they are experts.

Finally, without taking anything away from the fact that in some secular contexts it may still be possible for popular piety to be a genuine expression of faith for some people, we cannot fail to point out how it could also become the best way for some to yield to secularization.[50] In fact, one of its features is to be found not only in the autonomy of the various social spheres (economy, politics, arts, human affection, religion ...)[51] but – especially in a late modern age like ours – in confining religion to the margins of real life. In contexts of this kind, popular piety can also be what remains of a world subjected to a utilitarian kind of logic and be an escape from it. So it is clear how, in such a context, popular piety could end up being the expression of a marginalized faith rather than being the expression of an inculturated faith.

---

50 In this regard, the distinction Angelini invites us to make may be appropriate, when he notes that "inscribing Christianity in the cultural code of a people is something different from popular piety. It is a decidedly more comprehensive reality.' G ANGELINI, Evangelii gaudium. *La conversione pastorale e la teologia*, in *Teologia* 39 (2014/4), 493-508, 507.

51 See the perceptive interpretation of secularization offered by N LUHMANN, *Funzione della religione,* Morcelliana, Brescia 1991.

Therefore, seriously accepting the perspective of the one people of God existing among different peoples also means asking how we deal with evidence for the importance of popular piety for the Church which comes from within very different cultural contexts from those of Latin America or the so-called south of the world.

Chapter 3
AN EXTROVERTED CHURCH
A CHURCH THAT EXISTS FOR OTHERS

We would not fully grasp the core of Francis' ecclesiology if we omitted to put his vision of a missionary Church going forth at the forefront. Here we come to terms with the most relevant and probably original aspect of the ecclesiology underlying his magisterium.

In this case too we are not dealing with an 'absolute beginning'. We know that the last Council had already offered a clearly renewed understanding of the Church's mission despite a view of Church which could have seen mission as something that had already been realized or which at the very least, concerned just certain places (so-called 'mission posts') and people (male and female missionaries). The renewed outlook of the Council recalled first of all how the Church – the concrete people of God – was itself the result of the divine mission. The Church is the beginning of the unification of humanity, the first effect of the sending of the Son, and of the Spirit carrying out the Father's work (cf. *Lumen Gentium*, 2-4, *LG*). This allowed us to see how fidelity to this origin could only lead to the Church being missionary in its structure. The Council text which puts this most succinctly is, in all probability, *Ad Gentes* (*AG*) 2. 'The pilgrim Church is missionary by her very nature, since it is from the mission of the Son and the mission of the Holy

Spirit that she draws her origin, in accordance with the decree of God the Father.'

It was also able to point to the contribution that was beginning to come from countries of ancient Christianity, within which it was possible to glimpse the need to re-evangelize categories of people for whom the Church was becoming more and more alien. In these contexts it was clearly about doing what Francis has now described as 'a re-reading of the gospel in the light of contemporary culture.'[1] Among the effects of such a re-reading, was conceiving of the Church as the universal sacrament of salvation and seeing how the one mission would be accomplished in different ways in different socio-anthropological contexts. Mission in places not yet reached by proclamation of the gospel is something else again, and yet another mission is to contexts which are formally already Christian. A text like *AG* 6 is particularly relevant to all this.

There is no doubt that reflection on the Council has seen further development at both the theological level and the level of the Magisterium.[2] With regard to the Magisterium, *Evangelii Nuntiandi* (*EN*) by Paul VI deserves a special

---

1 Cf. A SPADARO, *Interview with Pope Francis*, cit.

2 At the theological level, in the Italian context, one thinks of all the important research and reflection carried out by Severino Dianich. Cf. for example, S DIANICH, *Chiesa in missione. Per una ecclesiologia dinamica*, Paoline, Cinisello Balsamo (MI) 1987; S DIANICH, *Chiesa estroversa. Una ricerca sulla volta dell'ecclesiologia contemporaneia*, Paoline, Cinisello Balsamo (MI) 1987. Mention also needs to be made of the recent manual prepared with Serena Noceti: S DIANICH – S NOCETI, *Trattato sulla Chiesa*, Queriniana, Brescia 2002.

mention here because of the great impact it had on the Latin American Church and of the great importance it has for the thinking of Jorge Bergoglio.[3] The issue was explored more deeply and contextualized in Latin America, as shown by reading the Aparecida Document, and we know that Bergoglio crucially contributed to the drawing up of this document and that today it flows into Francis' papal magisterium.[4]

Starting out from these premises, then, we can understand how Francis' discourse on the missionary Church going forth can be particularly trenchant and rich for Churches in areas that were Christian from ancient times and are today marked by dechristianization and secularization. What was beginning to be obvious prior to the Council and during it is taken for granted today: also and even especially in these places, a new evangelization is urgent and cannot be put off any longer.

It is when we read it primarily in this context that the proposal contained in the Pope's teaching becomes especially stimulating.

---

3 Cf. CM Galli. *Il forte vento del Sud*, cit., 59-60. In his address to participants in the Rome Diocesan Conference in 2014, Francis said of *EN*: "Still to this day it is the most important post-Conciliar pastoral document, which hasn't been surpassed. We should always go back to it. That Apostolic Exhortation is a great source of inspiration ... And it hasn't been surpassed. It is a wealth of resources for pastoral life." FRANCIS, *Address to participants at the Rome Diocesan Conference* entitled: '*A people who generates its children, communities and families in the great stages of Christian initiation*', Monday 16 June 2014.

4 Cf. CM GALLI, *La riforma missionaria della Chiesa secondo Francesco*, cit., 41.

1. *We are all missionary disciples: those who proclaim and the gospel that is proclaimed*

For Francis, the Church's mission clearly responds to the mandate from the Risen Lord which we find at the end of Matthew's Gospel, where Christ sends his disciples to preach the gospel in every time and place (Mt 28:19-20).[5] The most profound reason, nevertheless, for which the Church is called to go forth is the result of the missionary initiative of the merciful God who was the first to go forth. In this respect what Francis says at the beginning of the first chapter of *Evangelii Gaudium* (*EG*) is particularly poignant. He says:

> An evangelizing community knows that the Lord has taken the initiative, he has loved us first (cf. 1 Jn 4:19), and therefore we can move forward, boldly take the initiative, go out to others, seek those who have fallen away, stand at the crossroads and welcome the outcast. Such a community has an endless desire to show mercy, the fruit of its own experience of the power of the Father's infinite mercy.[6]

This passage reminds us of two essential aspects of Francis' ecclesiological teaching.

In the first place, it is not just any Church person who is the missionary but the entire community which is called the 'evangelizing community'. It is the Church as such

5 *EG*, no. 19.
6 *Ibidem*, no. 24.

which is called to evangelize; along with each individual within it. This is clearly connected to the notion that the Church is the people of God among which all Christians are gifted with equal dignity as sons and daughters and are equally responsible, united as they are by the Spirit. From this perspective we cannot maintain that evangelization is simply up to one or other individual. If the people of God is missionary by nature, then it follows that every Christian is too. Indeed, being a disciple of Christ and being a missionary cannot be separated from one another. The Pope states this essential connection between being disciples and being evangelizers in the original text by hyphenating the term: *discepoli-missionari* [translated in the official English text, however, as "missionary disciples" in inverted commas to indicate that it is a composite term]. He says: 'Every Christian is a missionary to the extent that he or she has encountered the love of God in Christ Jesus: we no longer say that we are "disciples" and "missionaries", but rather that we are always "missionary disciples."'[7]

The above passage is also illuminating for grasping the aim of proclamation. What the Church is called to proclaim is the gospel of mercy that gives it its existence, from which it lives and by which it is constantly evangelized. It is an aspect we should highlight, not only to grasp how there is a clear link, in Francis' teaching, between the mass recovery of Divine Mercy and the Church going forth, but also to highlight how evangelization does not just take

---

7   *Ibidem*, no. 120.

place through mere verbal proclamation.[8] Evangelization and human advancement, while distinct, cannot be seen as separate: the Church's commitment to the advancement and flourishing of humanity has to do with a gospel, at the centre of which is the God who has the miseries of humanity, sin included, very much at heart. Based on the magisterium of his predecessor, Francis therefore invites us to consider how charity is not foreign to the evangelizing work of the Church. 'From the heart of the Gospel' he says 'we see the profound connection between evangelization and human advancement, which must necessarily find expression and develop in every work of evangelization.'[9] He quotes from the Motu proprio *Intima Ecclesia natura* by Pope Benedict XVI to state that '"the service of charity is also a constituent element of the Church's mission and an indispensable expression of her very being." By her very nature the Church is missionary; she abounds in effective charity and a compassion which understands, assists and promotes.'[10] We understand, therefore, why the Pope often invites the Church to be at the peripheries or not to be afraid of being a 'field hospital'.

They are metaphors that risk becoming slogans detracting from the profundity of Francis' proposal, if we do not frame them this way. The duty that the Church has of bending over all the wounds of humanity and working to see that

8 This is a feature which is especially stressed in Latin American theology: cf. J Sobrino, *Gesù Cristo liberatore*, cit., 154-155.
9 *EG*, no. 178.
10 *Ibidem*, no. 179.

no one is rejected, discarded does not come from some kind of neutral philanthropy: it is a requirement of the gospel of mercy which it is called to proclaim.

Precisely because it is a proclamation of God's heart bending over wretchedness – including sin and every division among human beings – it cannot be reduced to the relationship of the individual with God[11] or to something that refers to an afterlife that has nothing to do with the here and now of the often wretched lives of human beings. The Pope clarifies this by highlighting the social significance of evangelization,[12] noting how the gospel implies the reign of God in the world, thus allowing social life to become 'a setting for universal fraternity, justice, peace and dignity'[13] and distancing itself from a view of Christianity that sees itself as a religion that deals with people's inner sanctum without involving an active commitment to transfiguring human society and all its institutions.[14]

It is clear that such a rethinking of the missionary nature of the Church can turn out to be a particularly promising path for the Churches of ancient Christianity and inhabitants of social contexts in which a certain post-modern ideology and secularization can see the relegation of faith to the sphere of the private and personal.[15] In the same way, in contexts where

11 Cf. *Ibidem*, no. 180.

12 Cf. especially *ibidem*, nos 176-185. He says explicitly in *EG*, no. 180: "Both Christian preaching and life, then, are meant to have an impact on society."

13 *Ibidem*, no. 180.

14 Cf. *Ibidem*, no. 183.

15 Cf. what the Pope himself says in *ibidem*, no. 64.

Christianity seems to be coming to an end, where the gospel message has already been heard and is often just taken for granted, and where there is a loss of dignity for many people, a Church that shows how evangelization implies witness and commitment to active processes of making the world more human can be especially effective.

2. *Mission and pastoral conversion*

A missionary Church going forth does mean, however, a *pastoral conversion*.

Right from the outset of *EG* the Pope makes it clear that taking up the notion of the Church as the community of missionary disciples who take the initiative to offer the gospel of Divine Mercy that they live by, means also engaging in pastoral conversion at all levels of ecclesial life: things cannot remain as they are. In this case too it is clear how this is based on the idea that the Church is the people of God animated and led by the Spirit so that each and every individual can be brought into contact with God's mercy: the root for this is a given, namely, the perspective of a dynamic, structured collective subject. We could similarly say that from a Church which is missionary by nature comes the duty of ceaseless pastoral conversion. Hence, Francis says: 'I hope that all communities will devote the necessary effort to advancing along the path of a pastoral and missionary conversion which cannot leave things as they presently are. "Mere administration" can no longer be enough. Throughout the world, let us be "permanently in a state of mission."'[16]

---

16   *Ibidem*, no. 25. Cf. *Ibidem*, nos 25-33.

This conversion concerns, especially, the ability to make the heart of the gospel clear once more in proclamation, namely: '... the beauty of the saving love of God made manifest in Jesus Christ.'[17]

It is such an important reminder but also one that is easily misunderstood. It is essential for a Church, such as is the case for the Western Church at a time when Christianity is dwindling, that wants to proclaim the gospel in a setting where Christianity can no longer be taken for granted. This is the situation where the heart of the gospel needs to be made clear again. And not just this: it is a question of seeing that this christological, trinitarian centre which involves every individual's freedom can never in any circumstance be taken for granted or as having already been achieved. Francis makes this clear when he talks about such proclamation as being the first: ' ... This first proclamation is called "first" not because it exists at the beginning and can then be forgotten or replaced by other more important things. It is first in a qualitative sense because it is the principal proclamation, the one which we must hear again and again in different ways, the one which we must announce one way or another throughout the process of catechesis, at every level and moment.'[18]

At the same time, this is a reminder that in the wake of the Council and from the perspective of a missionary Church, there is a 'hierarchy of truths'. Truths, especially moral ones, revolve around this centre and in relation to it.

17 *Ibidem*, no. 36.
18 *Ibidem*, no. 164.

We can in no way interpret Francis' invitation as leading to a lessening of the integrity of the gospel and of truth. Rather is it an invitation to rediscover the heart of the gospel which consists in the salvific encounter with Christ and, therefore, with the love of God, so that every truth can be rediscovered and integrated within the right perspective.[19]

Thinking in particular of Churches called to receive this invitation within their context of secularization and dwindling Christianity, there are a number of things here that could be explored.[20] But given the need to be brief, I will mention four especially urgent ones: restructuring Christian communities on the basis of the need to proclaim the gospel to those who do not know about it or have an erroneous perception of it; setting up places of genuine fraternity; the preferential choice of the young; real and responsible involvement of the laity.

Consideration needs to be given first of all to the fact that too often, Christian communities in places where Christianity is well-established are still structured around the hypothesis that they are 'normal Christian' groups where the faith is passed on in the families people come from,

19 Cf. A Cozzi, *La verità di Dio e dell'uomo in Cristo*, cit., 14-22.
20 For a rethinking of Church in this context cf. R Repole, *Come stelle in terra. La Chiesa nell'epoca della secolarizzazione*, Cittadella, Assisi 2012; and for a reconsideration of some of the fundamental questions regarding the Christian faith within contemporary culture, cf. G Ferretti, *Il grande compito. Tradurre la fede nello spazio pubblico secolare*, Cittadella, Assisi 2013; G Ferretti, *Spiritualità cristiana nel mondo contemporaneo. Per un superamento della mentalità sacrificale*, Cittadella, Assisi 2016.

where Christian life can count on the support of a social context which passes on Christian values. So much energy is spent maintaining the *status quo*, and as a result fewer resources are available for proclaiming the gospel to those who, for various reasons, have a distorted perception of it. The Pope's invitation should give rise to energy and pastoral imagination for restructuring communities in such a way that the main resources are used in this direction.

Closely connected with this is the need for Christian communities to be places where Christians can deal with their faith, before being places of choice for carrying out initiatives. In a context where it can no longer be taken for granted that people are Christian, and where believers live in the presence of other people who are unbelievers,[21] it is more necessary than ever to compare our faith with other believers, just as it is essential to have experiences of genuine Christian fraternity.

A third aspect that should be noted concerns the need for pastoral care that makes a genuine preferential choice at different levels for young people. The 'normal' communication of faith we could count on in a Christian

---

21 The reference is to the important understanding of secularization offered by Charles Taylor. He goes beyond the interpretation of secularization as the inevitable withdrawal of the religious person faced with the advances made by the modern world. Rather is secularization to be understood as a change of condition for belief; as the possibility of believing given the equally plausible and opposite possibility of unbelief and an "exclusive humanism". Cf. C TAYLOR, *A Secular Age,* Harvard University Press, September 2007.

environment has clearly been interrupted in their case.[22] It is to them that a Christian community should feel called, in the first instance, to proclaim the novelty of Christ with all the poignancy of this that we have already spoken about; not looking at the situation youth are in as a kind of 'disease'; and not thinking of being able to do something about it through events which divert attention from the commitment to forming consciences, seeing to growth and acting in such a way that in the Spirit, Christ can reach their hearts and light up their faces.

Finally, it is obvious that pastoral conversion must also and especially involve a declericalization of the Church which implies the effective recognition of the essential contribution of all Christians, and obviously lay Christians in particular, so that the gospel is proclaimed in a way that involves the close connection between proclamation and real charity, and reaches as many men and women as possible.

3. *Lay involvement*

For the importance it has, and for the slant it takes on in Francis' ecclesiological thinking, it is worth pausing to look at how the Pope himself considers the role of the laity in a Church which goes forth.

In the context of what has already been mentioned about the Church as the people of God. Francis has insisted, since *EG*, on the importance of recovering the meaning and practice of active lay involvement. He does so in

---

22   Cf., for example, F GARRELLI, *Piccoli atei crescono. Davvero una generazione senza Dio?*, Il Mulino, Bologna 2016.

particular by signalling how among the ecclesial challenges that a missionary Church going forth must tackle is that of remembering that 'Lay people are, put simply, the vast majority of the people of God. The minority – ordained ministers – are at their service.'[23] That the recovery of their prominence and activity represents a challenge has been reiterated by him more recently, and ironically, when he recalled how often it has been said that the hour of the laity has struck, but no real ecclesial transformation has followed; 'For example,' Francis said 'I recall now the famous phrase: "It is the hour of the laity", but it seems that the clock has stopped."[24]

To highlight the specific nature of the Pope's language in this regard, it is important to note that he takes what we have gained from the second chapter of *LG* absolutely for granted, where it is clear that we cannot think there is as Church *ad intra* which is the prerogative of the clerics, and a Church *ad extra* which is the prerogative of the laity. All equally belong to the people of God and are responsible for its mission. Nevertheless, without pointing to any systematic theological development of the question and in no way impairing this view, he lets us glimpse how we also need to recover one of the aspects that the 'secular nature' of the laity, mentioned in Chapter Four of *LG*, intended to safeguard: the fact that the Church exists for others, that it is missionary, that is

---

23 *EG*, no. 102. Cf. E Palladino, *I laici: l'immensa maggioranza del popolo di Dio*, in HM Yañez (ed.), Evangelii gaudium: *Il testo interroga*, cit., 67-80, 76-77.

24 Francis, *Il santo popolo fedele di Dio*, cit., 202.

called to live in and transfigure the realities of this world. The reasons why active involvement of the laity has been hindered, according to Francis, are instructive: the fact that they were not given proper formation; the fact of not having found room to speak and act in their particular Churches; but also the fact that they have often been called to take on tasks within the Church to the detriment of a commitment to evangelization which transforms society.[25]

Beyond a complete theological discussion of this issue, we have to at least admit that Francis' perspective is an invitation not only to recognize that the Church is mostly made up of lay Christians, that its ministers are at the service of this majority and that there is a fraternal bond that exists between both, but also that the Church is going forth to where there are already lay people who live and transmit the gospel to the world. Any talk about the laity risks being incomplete if it does not recognize this as an essential factor for being Church. From this comes the awareness that the Church does not only exist when it meets together but also where, due especially to the Christian laity, it is alive in this world's realities. This awareness should then be an encouragement for pastoral conversion (and even for the Code of Canon Law) to see that there are places (for example, groups or bodies where people can participate) for listening to the richness but also the tensions experienced by so many Christians when they proclaim the gospel by meeting people, at work, in their various professions, looking after the weak, helping children to grow, tackling social issues.

25 *Ibidem*, no. 129. Cf. *Ibidem*, nos 127-129.

4. *A style that is also its content*

On the basis of what has been said thus far, both in relation to the proclamation (the gospel of mercy), or to those responsible for it (all Christians and primarily the majority made up of the laity), it should be no surprise that Francis points out how the Church's mission is to be realized in person-to-person relationships.

It would be absurd to think of 'mass evangelization', precisely because it is the gospel of mercy that is being proclaimed, which must touch people in their individual and unique circumstances, and which is an appeal to their free, personal response and cannot be reduced to just verbal communication. It implies effective charity and finally, is transmitted by counting on the multiple charisms of all Christians (laity in the first instance). It always takes place through personal encounter. Hence there are many ways of evangelizing: 'This communication takes place in so many different ways that it would be impossible to describe or catalogue them all, and God's people, with all their many gestures and signs, are its collective subject.'[26]

This tells us how important the style of proclamation is, to the extent of saying that the style already expresses the content. It implies a relationship and genuine encounter between the one making the proclamation and the one receiving it.

And it is from this perspective that we must also interpret Francis' teaching style involving a clear change in

---

26 *Ibidem*, no. 129. Cf. *Ibidem*, nos 127-129.

magisterial language,[27] as well as the teachings given to those who are invested with the task of authoritative proclamation from among the people of God. Using language that aims to involve the listener/reader, which looks for every way possible to be at that person's level, and which searches for metaphors relevant to life, Francis shows, in fact, how even magisterial language can and should normally be a pastoral language, as it is aimed at evangelization. These are the terms for understanding the great importance given by Francis to the homily as his normal way of exercising his personal teaching as Bishop of Rome.[28] At the same time, it is precisely on the homily, its preparation and its effectiveness that the Pope insists when he addresses pastors:[29] a sign of the importance that the communication of faith from person to person

---

27 Cf. what C Theobald has to say, *Fraternità. Il nuovo stile della chiesa secondo papa Francesco*, Qiqajon, Magnano (BI) 2016, 20-25. Cf. also M Semeraro, *Introduzione*, in Francesco, Evangelii gaudium. *Esortazione apostolica*, San Paolo, Cinisello Balsamo (MI) 2013, 7-27, 11-12.

28 See what is highlighted in this regard by S Dianich, *Magistero in movimento. Il caso papa Francisco*, Dehoniane, Bologna 2016, 35-66. And again, the novelty of language closely associated with gestures is remarked upon by DE Viganò, *Fedeltà e cambiamento. La svolta di Francesco raccontato da vicino*, Rai-Eri, Rome 2015, 103-124.

29 See the great relevance this topic assumes in *EG*, nos 135-159. Consider in particular how Francis highlights the importance of the personalized word on the part of the preacher, so that he is totally involved in what he proclaims and is witness to (nos 149-151); and the need for him to also listen to the people so his word can reach those who listen to him (nos 154-155). Cf. also G Ravasi, *Una vera "Postfazione". L'omelia secondo papa Francesco*, in A Cozzi – R Repole – G Piana, *Papa Francesco. Quale teologia?*, cit., 193-208.

must also have for them, since the homily is a form of live communication where real people are involved and in which the relationship created between the speaker and the listener is fundamental.

This emphasis is not to be interpreted as any kind of repudiation of more 'definitive' or 'dogmatic' language when the authenticity of the faith risks being compromised. Rather does it signal how the latter cannot be the language normally used for passing on the faith; and he reminds us how, in every case, it always requires the personal involvement of the believer.

But because people do not exist outside of a culture, the Church's mission always implies, for Francis, an inculturation and evangelization of culture. It is interesting how the Pope interprets this – through the category of openness, acceptance; as if evangelizing a culture means that the Church has to be open in some of its dimensions. In fact he says: 'When certain categories of reason and the sciences are taken up into the proclamation of the message, these categories then become tools of evangelization; water is changed into wine.'[30] It should be noted that, even without mentioning him, Francis uses the same example here employed by Thomas to defend himself from those who accused him of watering down the gospel with his theology, because of his use of reason and philosophy.[31] In the same way, we need to point out that Francis sees theology as the

30   *EG*, no. 132.
31   Cf. THOMAS, *Expositio super librum Boetii de Trinitate*, q.2, art. 3, ob. 5, and ad 5. Cf. what Chenu says about the dynamics of

essential tool for carrying out this inculturation on the part of a missionary Church going forth.[32]

It is clear how such a change of style also has to be a part of pastoral conversion, especially for a Church living within Western culture. Very succinctly, it could be useful to point to three contexts for conversion in such a setting, in order to genuinely take up the perspectives presented by the Pope.

The first concerns the need to move from a Church that could depend on 'mass Christianity' to a Church which now structures itself in the knowledge that the gospel can only be transmitted from person to person. This once again needs to be spelt out as the ability to discern, foster and value the charisms of so many lay Christians who normally proclaim the gospel through interpersonal encounters in their various life contexts; and in the ability to make room for those who welcome the gospel with faith and enter the Church, bringing their freshness, uniqueness and individuality to it. In this sense, the emphasis on the Church's missionary outlook must go hand in hand with the emphasis on synodality, which will be discussed later.

The second is with regard to the importance theology now has for this. Without a real appreciation of the work of theology, the Church will hardly be able to make the gospel audible and inculturate it in our late modern or postmodern culture. Think, just by way of example, how much theological effort is needed for the gospel to really be proclaimed in a

---

purification and illumination that such transformation wrought in Thomas: MD CHENU, *La teologia come scienza nel XII secolo*, Jaca Book, Milan 1995, 123-125.

32 Cf. *EG*, nos 133-134.

culture dominated by science and disenchantment with the world.

Finally, the task of evangelizing culture means, for Churches in generally democratic Western societies, *having the ability to occupy the public space while no longer depending on a position of strength and power* and without at the same time abdicating its role in offering the transfiguring power of the gospel in bringing about a more just and fraternal society.[33] To do this, Christians must be capable of showing, in public discourse, the humanizing power of gospel values; and of being ready to work within the normal democratic approaches to convince people who are not Christian of the humanizing impact of these values.

This is something that Pope Francis clearly has very much at heart.

5. *The prophetic dimension of proclamation: denouncing practical relativism*

For Francis, any rethinking of a missionary Church going forth today has to be accompanied by denouncing the idolatries which characterize our late modern and

---

33 In order to grasp how secularization also marks the public space and to be aware of the changes this implies for a Church which does not want to abdicate its role in proclaiming the gospel in this context, it could be useful to read M Gauchet, *Un mondo disincantato? Tra laicismo e riflusso clericale*, edizioni Dedalo, Bari 2008; M Gauchet, *La religione nella democrazia*, edizioni Dedalo, Bari 2009. See, also, L Diotallevi, *Fine corsa. La crisi del cristianesimo come religione confessionale*, Dehoniane, Bologna 2017. For an ecclesiological reflection along these lines, cf. S Dianich, *Chiesa e laicità dello Stato*, San Paolo, Cinisello Balsamo (BI) 2011.

globalized world: especially the idolatry of money[34] and the idolatry which can be found in the mythical exaltation of technology.[35]

At first they might look like two unrelated things but in truth they are closely connected: the Church could not proclaim the gospel of mercy from which it has its existence without at the same time denouncing the idols which pretend to take the place of the God revealed to us in Christ and who is alive in the Spirit. They end up dehumanizing humanity and disintegrating the earth. The Pope sheds light on the idolatry of money which underlies economic liberalism and gives birth to economic injustice which dehumanizes both the victims and those who produce it. The same applies to the 'technocratic paradigm',[36] which ends up destroying our common home at the expense first of all of the life and dignity of the very poor.[37]

As the voice of a Church that is missionary and because

---

34 Cf. *Ibidem*, nos 55-56. For an examination of idolatry and its mythical dimensions cf. R REPOLE, *Annuncia del Vangelo e idolatria*, in M GRONCHI – R REPOLE, *Il dolce stil novo di papa Francesco*, cit., 49-88, 80-88. Cf. G Piana, *Il magistero morale di papa Francesco*, in A COZZA – R REPOLE – G PIANA, *Papa Francesco. Quale teologia?*, cit., 127-191. 148-156. On the importance of the theme in the theological ambit, cf. D Marguerat, *Dio e il denaro*, Qiqajon, Magnano (BI) 2104; D-R DUFOUR, *Le divin Marché. La révolution culturelle libérale*, Denoel, Paris 2007.

35 See especially Chapter 3 of *LS* dedicated to discerning the causes of the ecological crisis.

36 Cf. *Ibidem*, nos 107-109.

37 Cf. *Ibidem*, nos 48-52. The extent that this theme shows up in Francis' life and his various addresses is pointed out in DE VIGANÒ, *Fedeltà a cambiamento. La svolta di Francesco raccontata da vicino*, cit., 125-132.

of this, capable of prophecy, Francis denounces especially the grave danger represented by practical relativism.[38] Benedict XVI, coming from the heart of a Europe which is undergoing a crisis of values and is suspicious of any perspective of truth, had opportunely stressed the anti-evangelical and dehumanizing power of theoretical relativism. Francis, coming from a Latin America where social inequality is more evident and who has been led to see the world from the point of view of the poor and the victim, today stresses the equally anti-evangelical and dehumanizing capacity of practical relativism. The study he offers of this phenomenon is extensive, precise and beneficially disquieting. Francis says:

> The culture of relativism is the same disorder which drives one person to take advantage of another, to treat others as mere objects, imposing forced labour on them or enslaving them to pay their debts. The same kind of thinking leads to the sexual exploitation of children and abandonment of the elderly who no longer serve our interests. It is also the mindset of those who say: Let us allow the invisible forces of the market to regulate the economy, and consider their impact on society and nature as collateral damage. In the absence of objective truths or sound principles other than the satisfaction of our own desires and immediate needs, what limits can be placed on human trafficking, organized crime, the drug trade, commerce

---

38   Cf. *EG*, no. 80.

> in blood diamonds and the fur of endangered species? Is it not the same relativistic logic which justifies buying the organs of the poor for resale or use in experimentation, or eliminating children because they are not what their parents wanted?[39]

It is clear that by virtue of the gospel from which it exists and which it is called to proclaim, the Church must be a prophetic voice, both with regard to theoretical relativism, and practical relativism. It will thus also express its 'critical reservations' regarding the postmodern, globalized world as it does for any culture. There is, however, a specific feature of practical relativism which has remarkable ecclesiological relevance. It can worm its way even into Christians whose doctrinal stance is indisputable and, says Francis, can affect ' … some who clearly have solid doctrinal and spiritual convictions'[40] but who can end up living as if God did not exist or making decisions as if there were no poor people. It is therefore possible to be Christians, profess correct spiritual doctrine and ideas, and yet fall into this kind of relativism.

This is why Francis believes it is even more dangerous than doctrinal relativism: it is a subtle threat which can end up with the community of believers in Christ speaking about the gospel without being evangelical. Hence conversion is as essential as the reformation of the Church; an ongoing, never-ending task.

---

39 *LS*, no. 123. See also the preceding number, 122.
40 *EG*, no. 80.

Chapter 4
THE NECESSARY REFORM

Fifty years on from Vatican II, it is rather clear today how the Council's texts are not always unambiguous in how they envisage the Church's transformation, including at the structural level, and that the reform of certain ecclesial institutions which many expected to happen following the Council has not yet been put in place.

Looking at Pope Francis' ecclesiological teaching and some of his important choices, it is obvious that we have entered a new phase of the reception of Vatican II in this respect as well. Being able to take advantage of the theological development prior to the Council and following it, he offers clear ideas and makes precise choices for reform.

As already noted, reform of the Church for Francis is not just any structural change. It is needed for the Church, with the passing of time and in changing situations, to remain always gospel-inspired and transparent, so that the merciful God who inhabits it and makes it exist shines through. In the light of what has been highlighted so far, it should be equally clear how reform, for this precise reason, is closely connected to the idea of a missionary Church going forth. The Church warns of the duty to go forth and to see that everyone encounters the merciful God who spoke ultimately in Christ and the gift of his Spirit. It knows it exists by virtue of the mercy of a God who took the initiative and was the first to go forth.¹ The Pope says this very clearly in the first chapter of *EG*: 'The renewal of structures demanded by pastoral conversion can only be understood in this light: as part of an effort to make them more mission-oriented, to make ordinary pastoral activity on every level more inclusive and open, to inspire in pastoral workers a constant desire to go forth and in this way to elicit a positive response from all those whom Jesus summons to friendship with himself.'²

In this case too we must not expect a program of systematic reform from the Pope, offered in any comprehensive way. At the same time, it is good to stress how Francis seems to trust in and act *according* to the kind of logic he often points out to Christians – not occupying spaces but setting processes in motion.

Because of this it is probably impossible and even insensitive to describe a precise framework of reforms that need to be put in place. To do so would ultimately mean contradicting some of the cornerstones of Francis' ecclesiological vision, some already mentioned and others we will need to look at: the fact, for example, that the Church is a dynamic entity guided by the living presence of the Spirit of Christ; the fact that all Christians are living and active subjects in the Church; the fact that local Churches are not administrative departments but Churches in their own right.

Just the same, we can identify some fundamental directions for reform in Francis' teaching owed to the

1 Cf. *EG*, no. 24.
2 *Ibidem*, no. 27.

ecclesiological stance thus far presented, and which are clearly interconnected. These concern: the synodality of the Church and overcoming a universalist view of Church; the importance of an intermediate collegiality; the papacy and the reality of the Synod of Bishops.

1. *Synodality and overcoming a universalist view of Church*

It is necessary to honestly recognize how the ecclesiological issue of synodality has come back into the limelight so forcefully with Francis' papacy. It was not a specific subject of debate at Vatican II, though in the ecclesiological vision of the people of God and the resulting notion of the *sensus fidei* there were already the premises for its development. In recent years, however, the topic for some has even been a suspect one.[3]

Francis has brought it back to the centre of ecclesial and ecclesiological attention. One address he gave which has by now become fundamental for his view of Church is especially instructive in this regard, and it clarifies how, for the Pope, synodality is the way to go in today's world because it brings about synergy in view of the Church's mission.[4] On the occasion of the 50th anniversary of the institution

---

3 We need to indicate that the Italian Theological Association has already had something to say about this, dedicating a Congress to it some years back: cf. Associazione Teologica Italiana, *Chiesa e sinodalità. Coscienza, forme, processi*, Glossa, Milan 2007. Cf. more recently, G RUGGIERI, *Chiesa sinodale*, Laterza, Bari 2017.

4 FRANCIS, *Address on the occasion of the 50th anniversary of the institution of the Synod of Bishops*. Saturday, 17 October 2015. see beginning of this address.

of the Synod of bishops on 17 October 2015, the Pope spoke of 'synodality as a constitutive element of the Church' following what John Chrysostom says about Church and synod being synonymous because, as Francis continues, 'the Church is nothing other than the "journeying together" of God's flock along the paths of history towards the encounter with Christ the Lord …'[5] The foundation for this is that the Church is the people of God; that all Christians are united in the Spirit and therefore there is a *sensus fidei* which makes the Church infallible *in credendo*; and that there can be no rigid separation between an *Ecclesia docens* and an *Ecclesia discens*. No one can be placed above the others within the Church. Anyone who takes on ministry in the Church is at the service of the others. The Pope is not afraid to speak of the Church using the image of an inverted pyramid, since 'the top is located beneath the base.'[6]

What we need to remind ourselves of here, above all, is that for the *sensus fidei* to be truly perceived there is a need (according to the Pope) to listen, and this needs to happen at all levels and in all individuals in the Church: in the awareness that listening is more than simply hearing, as he suggests with anthropological finesse:[7] 'A synodal Church is a Church which listens, which realizes that listening "is more than simply hearing." It is a mutual listening in which everyone has something to learn. The faithful people,

  5 *Ibidem.*
  6 *Ibidem.*
  7 Cf. *EG* 171, where the Pope explains that listening is not complete passivity, inasmuch as it "helps us to find the right gesture and word which shows that we are more than simply bystanders."

the college of bishops, the Bishop of Rome: all listening to each other, and all listening to the Holy Spirit, the "Spirit of truth" (Jn14:17), in order to know what he "says to the Churches" (Rev 2:7).'[8]

Synodality is something, therefore, that has to happen at every level of the Church's life. It is essential for the voice of the Spirit to be heard, through listening to everyone.

This kind of language concerns reform insofar as it obliges us to ask ourselves where we are Church, or in other words, what is the first and most basic level for carrying out this mutual listening which is the basis of our journeying together.

We know how there was a clear restoration of the view at Vatican II that local Churches really are Churches and of the perspective that sees the Church as a *communio Ecclesiarum*.[9] It is also known how the recovery of such an ecclesiology took place within a still generally universalist framework of the Church. Symbolic of this is the fact that the college of bishops is still seen as something partly detached from the communion of Churches.[10] It must not, therefore, surprise

8   FRANCIS, *Address on the occasion of the 50th anniversary of the institution of the Synod of Bishops*. Saturday, 17 October 2015, cit.

9   A text able to show the importance and effects of this change compared with earlier ecclesiology is the one by H LEGRAND, *La réealisation de l'église en un lieu*, in B LAURET – F REFOULÉ (eds), *Initiation à la pratique de la théologie, III*, Cerf, Paris 1983, 145-345.

10   We see this in a critical reading of *LG* 22 when it is taken literally. It allowed for post-conciliar interpretations heading in this direction, such as is the case with *Apostolos suos*, no. 12, by John Paul II. Cf. J Legrande, Communio Ecclesiae, communio Ecclesiorum, collegium episcoporum, in A SPADARO – CM GALLI

us that in recent decades, following the document from the Congregation of the Doctrine of the Faith, *Communionis Notio*, stating an ontological and temporal precedence of the universal Church with respect to local Churches, there was an intense theological debate involving Ratzinger and Kasper. Francis seems to lean crucially toward the notion that we cannot understand the universality of the Church as a reality which comes before the concrete existence of local Churches.[11] The way in which he speaks of the particular Church in *EG* 30 is most significant. He says: 'Each particular Church, as a portion of the Catholic Church under the leadership of its bishop, is likewise called to missionary conversion. It is the primary subject of evangelization, since it is the concrete manifestation of the one Church in one specific place, and in it "the one, holy, catholic, and apostolic Church of Christ is truly present and operative."'[12] It should be noted that the Pope is talking about the local Church not as a part of, but a portion of the Church; and the reference, in a footnote, is to *Christus Dominus* (*CD*) 11, one of the most mature texts in which Vatican II regains and expresses a theology of the local Church.

(eds), *La Riforma e le riforme nella Chiesa*, cit., 159-188, 159-164.

11 Kasper notes how, in the question of the relationship between the universal Church and local Churches "Cardinal Bergoglio too, as Archbishop of Buenos Aires, occasionally found himself in conflict with positions taken by the Roman Curia. He is now taking up the matter within the framework of the ecclesiology of *communio* and speaks of a decentralization of the Church and a strengthening of Episcopal Conferences (*EG 16; 32*)." W KASPER, *Papa Francesco*, cit., 73.

12 *EG*, no. 30.

It should likewise not go unnoticed that during the Jubilee of Mercy, Francis asked that a holy door be opened in every particular Church,[13] and that the first door to be opened was in Africa.[14] These are all concrete signs saying that local Churches are not parts or districts of a universal Church considered in abstract terms as existing prior to them. Instead they are the Church insofar as it exists in a determined 'place', as emerges from the way Paul writes in his Letters (cf. 1 Cor 1:2; 2 Cor 1:1; 1 Thess 1:1).

Since there has been a recovery of the complete consistency of local Churches we can understand why, for the Pope, synodality has to take place at this level first, and implies the essential reform of the participatory bodies which each Church must make use of. It is worth recording what Francis says in his address regarding synodality and the Synod of bishops:

> The first level of the exercise of synodality is had in the particular Churches. After mentioning the noble institution of the Diocesan Synod, in which priests and laity are called to cooperate with the bishop for the good of the whole ecclesial community, the Code of Canon Law devotes ample space to what are usually called "organs of communion" in the local Church: the presbyteral council, the college of consultors, chapters of canons and the pastoral council.

---

13 Cf. FRANCIS, *Misericordiae Vultus*, no. 3.
14 Cf. DE VIGANÒ, *Fratelli e sorelle, funoasera. Papa Francesco e la comunicazione.* Carocci editore, Rome 2016, 143-144.

> Only to the extent that these organizations keep connected to the "base" and start from people and their daily problems, can a synodal Church begin to take shape: these means, even when they prove wearisome, must be valued as an opportunity for listening and sharing.[15]

The Pope's words demonstrate the awareness which is common to many today that these bodies have often gone through crisis and need to be revitalized. He refers to the Code of Canon Law and does not seem to be suggesting premeditated solutions. We can interpret his words from the perspective of the real subjectivity of every single local Church called to take its destiny into its own hands. It should be noted that there is a clear direction we can take from the Pope's words: these participatory bodies must not only be places for organizing activities *ad intra* since they must start out from the everyday problems that people experience; and they must not be just places where they listen, but also ones where they can share.

He does not talk about what they need to especially share but, in the light of the fundamental direction we find in Francis' ecclesiology, it would make sense to think that it would be mainly to do with the faith as lived and passed on in practice. To carry out genuine evangelization in a complex world, where faith exists alongside the possibility of non-belief as well, it is more essential than ever that believers discuss and mutually sustain their own faith and how they

---

15 FRANCIS, *Address on the occasion of the 50th anniversary of the institution of the Synod of Bishops.* Saturday, 17 October 2015, cit.

pass it on. Participatory bodies can and must increasingly become places for such exchange.

2. *Episcopal conferences and intermediate collegiality*

Given that each Church exists in *communio* with all the others and especially with the Church of Rome, which presides over them in charity (according to the well-known expression of Ignatius of Antioch), it follows that synodality has to be extended to other levels as well; and it must involve the bishops who preside over the Churches and who need to 'represent them'. Here we are talking about episcopal collegiality.

It is on this, and specifically at the level expressed by the term 'intermediate collegiality', that we seem to see Pope Francis' main efforts at reform.

It was a topic that was much debated in the decades following the Council. In spite of those who maintained that there would be an *effective* exercise of episcopal collegiality even in Episcopal Conferences in which only the bishops of a given territory took part, there were those, instead, who believed that an effective exercise of collegiality would occur only when all the bishops took part: in other cases there would only be *affective* collegiality. Assuming this last position, it would be practically impossible, however, to overcome strong centralization. From this it follows that – other than the Council, which remains an exception – we would end up with government by the pope regarding the universal Church, and by individual bishops regarding the local Church. Besides having to point out how such a view contradicts the practice of the ancient Church, it is worth noting how it would be less than helpful for a missionary Church needing intermediate decision-making to promote the proclamation of the gospel in Churches within cultures very different to one another.

Pope Francis clearly seems to head in the direction of decentralization and thus the enhancement of opportunities for intermediate collegiality because it relaunches a new phase of evangelization, in the hope that the gospel of mercy may encounter people in their individual circumstances and different cultures.[16] This obviously requires that discernment be made and decisions be taken by local episcopates and not delegated to Rome.[17] In the view of a missionary Church going forth, centralization is an obstacle instead of being a help. So we understand why, since *EG*, Francis has said he is in favour of the effective enhancement of intermediate collegiality when he said:

> The Second Vatican Council stated that, like the ancient patriarchal Churches, episcopal conferences are in a position "to contribute in many and fruitful ways to the concrete realization of the collegial spirit". Yet this desire has not been fully realized, since a juridical status

---

16 Cf. J XAVIER, *Spalancamento del dinamismo ecclesiale: l'identità ritrovata*, in HM YAÑEZ (ed.) Evangelii gaudium: *il testo interroga*, cit., 39-52, 46-49. This offers a clearer reception of what the Council Fathers hoped for in the final paragraph of AG 22 or AG 31, in the context of a reflection on the missionary nature of the Church.

17 Cf. *EG*, no. 16.

of episcopal conferences which would see them as subjects of specific attributions, including genuine doctrinal authority, has not yet been sufficiently elaborated. Excessive centralization, rather than proving helpful, complicates the Church's life and her missionary outreach.[18]

He returned to this issue in the above-mentioned address for the 50th anniversary of the Synod of Bishops; and he has shown that he clearly supports a reform in this direction by the fact that from the outset, in his documents, he not only quotes his predecessors but various interventions by different Episcopal Conferences as well.[19] He has thus shown his recognition of their real magisterium, wanting to give them real value; and he does not think of their ministry as a service to the unity of the Church apart from the actual reality of the Churches, in a new reception of what *LG* 13 said regarding the Petrine ministry. There it said that the Chair of Peter 'protects legitimate differences, while at the same time assuring that such differences do not hinder unity but rather contribute toward it.'

For someone who really has at heart a Church capable of evangelizing in today's world, which is clearly more globalized in economic terms but still characterized by different cultures, the importance of giving real value to Episcopal Conferences will obviously be important, as

18 *Ibidem*, no. 32.
19 Semeraro immediately noticed this in *EG*: cf. M SEMERARO, *Introduzione*, cit., 24-25. We see the same thing, just to give some examples, in *LS* 14; 38; 41; 48; 51; 52; 54.

well as creating new patriarchates, when needed, based on the distribution of Christians in the world today. This is a proposal, following the Council, that a refined ecclesiologist like Joseph Ratzinger had already put forward, but in fact it has remained a dead letter.[20]

Francis' pontificate at least has the merit of making this plausible once more, and with it, as is clearly the case, he has brought the question of a rethinking of the papacy itself to the fore.

3. *The Papacy and the Synod of bishops*

While we are limiting our attention to relatively recent times, we certainly cannot say that the need to bring about a reform involving the papacy is something completely new, either for theology or the magisterium.

In terms of theology we can recall, by way of example, the proposal Ratzinger put forward as a theologian – on the same occasion he expressed a wish for new patriarchates – to clearly distinguish, for the future, the office of the Successor of Peter from the office of the Patriarch.[21] In terms of the magisterium, instead, we need to mention the desire expressed by John Paul II in *Ut Unum Sint*, in nos 95-96, to set up a fraternal dialogue with those responsible for other Churches and their theologians with a view to finding a way of exercising the primacy that would be open to new

---

20 Cf. J RATZINGER, *Il nuovo popolo di Dio,* Queriniana, Brescia 1992, 155-156.
21 *Ivi.*

circumstances without renouncing its essential mission.[22]

Pope Francis is clearly moving in the same direction, and doing so decisively. Symptomatic of this could be the fact that on the very first evening of his election he presented himself to the Church with the title of Bishop of Rome, and he has often done so since. Something else that could be emblematic is the fact that over these years, through his gestures and way of presenting himself, he has tended toward a clear desacralization of his role. And it is also he himself who has expressly declared that he wants to give serious consideration to a reform of the papacy in the context of a missionary Church going forth. In *EG* he recognized that 'The papacy and the central structures of the universal Church also need to hear the call to pastoral conversion.'[23]

Many recognize that one of the symbolic and strategic places in which to intervene to this end would be the Roman Curia, so that it neither overrides individuals bishops nor Episcopal Conferences but is rather a help to them and the Pope. Francis has demonstrated his intention of bringing about real changes in this direction.[24] Setting up a council

---

[22] Someone who wanted to respond in a very significant way to John Paul II's request was O CLÉMENT, *Roma diversamente. Un ortodosso di fronte al papato*, Jaca Book, Milan 1998.

[23] *EG*, no. 32. Seeing the clear ecumenical significance of this and recognizing how much there is to be learned from our Orthodox brothers in terms of episcopal collegiality and synodality, Francis also said: "I want to continue the discussion that was begun in 2007 by the joint [Catholic–Orthodox] commission on how to exercise the Petrine primacy, which led to the signing of the Ravenna Document. We must continue on this path." A SPADARO, *Interview with Pope Francis*, cit.

[24] This is one of Francis' obvious wishes. He has said that "The

made up of cardinals has been an important choice in this regard and heralds beneficial consequences. But as well as being of help in governing the Church they need to support him in reforming the Curia.[25]

With regard to any real reform of the papacy, one of the fundamental institutions also demanding to be reformed is the Synod of bishops. Some dissatisfaction has been registered now for decades both regarding its importance and the procedures adopted.[26] From the beginning of his pontificate, Francis has not failed to say expressly that this is a fundamental institution but one which needs to change.[27] Yet he has not limited himself to just complaining about what is lacking; he has also put some significant changes

---

dicasteries of the Roman Curia are at the service of the pope and the bishops," he says. "They must help both the particular churches and the bishops' conferences. They are instruments of help. In some cases, however, when they are not functioning well, they run the risk of becoming institutions of censorship. It is amazing to see the denunciations for lack of orthodoxy that come to Rome. I think the cases should be investigated by the local bishops' conferences, which can get valuable assistance from Rome. These cases, in fact, are much better dealt with locally. The Roman congregations are mediators; they are not middlemen or managers." A SPADARO, *Interview with Pope Francis*, cit.

25   The Pope has also said that this was a decision made among the cardinals in the General Congregations before the Conclave. Cf. A SPADARO, *Interview with Pope Francis*, cit.

26   Cf., for example, A ANTÓN, *La collegialità nel Sinodo dei vescovi*, in J TOMKO (ed.), *Il Sinodo dei vescovi. Natura-Metodo-Prospettive*, LEV, Vatican City 1985, 59-111; and G ROUTHIER, *Le Synode des év~eques: un débat inachevé*, in G ROUTHIER – L VILLEMIN (eds), *Nouveaux apprentissages pour l'Église*, Cerf, Paris 2006, 269-293.

27   Cf. A SPADARO, *Interview with Pope Francis*, cit.

in place. By calling an extraordinary Synod preceded by wide consultation, followed by the ordinary Synod on the family in autumn 2015, he acted in such a way that the Synod would be better situated within the framework of a broader synodal process. 'Certainly', Francis said during the already mentioned address on the occasion of the 50th anniversary of the Synod of Bishops, 'a consultation of this sort would never be sufficient to perceive the *sensus fidei*. But how could we speak about the family without engaging families themselves, listening to their joys and their hopes, their sorrows and their anguish?'[28] This limitation, which the Pope himself has recognized, can help with recognizing one of the aspects that reform must take into consideration more objectively: the formalization of structures and processes which, without prejudice to the nature of a Synod of Bishops, will allow the entire people of God to be truly involved and will ensure that Christians who are more directly involved in matters dealt with from time to time can be made responsible.

The way in which Francis invites us to consider the Synod of bishops does, however, lead to an interpretation that involves the papacy itself. In the anniversary address previously mentioned, Francis spoke of the Synod as an expression of episcopal collegiality 'which can also become in certain circumstances "effective", joining the Bishops among themselves and with the Pope in solicitude for the People God.'

---

28 FRANCIS, *Address on the occasion of the 50th anniversary of the institution of the Synod of Bishops. Saturday, 17 October 2015*, cit.

This is an important statement, leading to an interpretation of the Synod as an expression of episcopal collegiality in which the bishops, with and under the pope, would exercise responsibility for governing the universal Church. The implications of this for the reform of ecclesial structures are considerable: up until now, both the Motu proprio *Apostolica Sollicitudo* of Paul VI with which the Synod of bishops was established, and the subsequent Council text *CD* 5, understood the Synod as being an aid to the pope's service of governing.[29]

Francis' words lead us to seeing him, instead, as an instrument of government by the bishops united with the pope on behalf of the universal Church: this is a direction for reform that incorporates the requests of those who, before and after the Council, have wanted to promote greater collegiality in the government of the Church.

---

29 A study seminar was held on this topic in the Vatican in 2016. Cf. L Baldisseri (ed.), *A cinquant'anni dall'*Apostolica Sollicitudo, *Il Sinodo dei vescovi al servizio di una Chiesa sinodale. Atti del Seminario di studio organizzato dalla Segreteria generale del Sinodo dei Vescovi (Città del Vaticano, 6-9 febbraio 2016)*, LEV, Vatican City 2016. Cf. A Indelicato, *Il Sinodo dei vescovi. La collegialità sospesa (1965-1985)*, Il Mulino, Bologna 2008.

EPILOGUE
BEING INVOLVED IN THE DREAM
TO REMAIN FAITHFUL TO THE GOSPEL

If Vatican II represents the opportunity for the Church, with the passing of time and in contact with modern culture, to rethink itself by mirroring itself in the perennial gospel, then Francis' pontificate, fifty years later, becomes a new opportunity for receiving and relaunching such rethinking.

The Church, thus mirrored, is the holy faithful people of God, whose perennial and inexhaustible source is the gospel of mercy centred on Christ and alive in the Spirit. From this special emphasis comes the possibility of a teaching that focuses on things that could sometimes be overlooked or neglected: the fact that the gospel must reach people in their unique circumstances, in their freedom, and within a certain culture, in a mutual (though asymmetrical) relationship with God, beginning with the poor and those most in need of mercy; the fact that the people of God is a dynamic entity made up of Christians endowed with equal dignity and shared responsibility; the fact that it is a people living among the different peoples of the earth; the fact that the *sensus fidei* expressed within this people is fundamental, more than just the ability to conceptualize Christian faith, and that it justifies giving renewed attention to the synodal dimension of the Church; the fact that this 'popular nature' of the Church cannot in any way be confused with any kind of 'populism'.

One effect of this special emphasis on a Church that is born of Divine Mercy as God's holy people, has been Francis' equally special relaunching of its missionary nature. The Church, as Mother, is called to make the gospel of mercy she lives by available everywhere, to everyone and to each individual. All Christians are responsible for this, since they are all missionary disciples. They are called to proclaim the gospel in so many different ways that they are impossible to categorize. This proclamation envisages a structurally different approach, a person-to-person one that depends on a number of factors: the differing and many charisms of those who do the proclaiming, the uniqueness of those who receive the gospel, the different cultures in which each one lives, the fact that the gospel can never be exhausted in an idea but – being the gospel of mercy – also implies a right way of going about it, an orthopraxis, overcoming any likely separation between the proclamation of the gospel, charity and human advancement.

From all this we understand how, for Francis, a missionary Church is a prophetic Church: because it is called to proclaim the gospel of mercy that has appeared definitively in Christ, it is also called to denounce all kinds of idolatry, thus taking a critical stance regarding not only doctrinal relativism, but also practical relativism which can worm its way even into the Church. At the same time, from all this comes the need for a Church in a constant state of conversion so that it may increasingly take on the form of the poor and merciful Christ, letting his gospel shine through and being constantly available to everyone; the need for a genuine reform of ecclesial structures is thus justified.

In the light of these ecclesiological perspectives as briefly summarized above, it is also clear how the reform must be oriented toward a decisive decentralization of the Church and truly overcome a universalist view of the Church. It must give local Churches a central role and see them as active subjects, must see the worth of intermediate episcopal collegiality and lead to a new interpretation of the Synod of bishops and the service of the papacy, making greater collegiality in the governance of the Church possible.

But the dream of a Church like this cannot just be the Pope's dream.

It demands that all Churches and all Christians get behind it. They are all involved, even though bearing different kinds of responsibility. In other words, it needs to be a shared dream based on a common and genuine evangelical passion and the real assumption of responsibility by everyone and every group in the Church.

Thinking, in particular, of the reform perspectives that the Pope proposes, we can hope that the dream involves Christians, pastors, theologians and canonists in rethinking, in particular, the structures of synodality within local Churches.

In fact, in the fifty years since the Council, much has been discussed and said about what was undoubtedly the central issue at the structural level for the Council Fathers: the relationship between the papacy and episcopal collegiality.

Today, it is clear how genuine reform asks for this turning point of the Council to be 'creatively received', focusing in particular on the level of local Churches: overcoming a 'monarchical' view of the ministry of bishops and priests; recovering the reality of the presbyterate and the novelty of the ministry of deacons;[1] rethinking participatory bodies so that the *sensus fidei* may actually be tapped; placing value on the different charisms and implementing genuine shared responsibility; a new appreciation of the diocesan Synod, where ordained and lay ministers work together, though with different roles, to assume responsibility for the fundamental pastoral choices of the Church to which they belong.[2]

These are but a few examples to say how the dream of a gospel-inspired Church given to us today through the

---

1   Cf. R Repole, *Il vescovo nel suo presbiterio. Ripensare oggi la realtà del presbiterio*, in *La Rivista del Clero Italiano*, 98 (2017/6), 405-419. Today we feel the need to go beyond the Council's texts, still based on the early model of Ignatius of Antioch, which came from a completely different ecclesial context. In this sense, it can be very instructive to appeal to other models of synodal ministry found in antiquity which rethink the reality of the episcopate and give consistency to the theme of the presbyterate, as well as being more responsive to the challenges that come from the complexity of current times. Cf. E Norelli, *La nascita del cristianesimo*, Il Mulino, Bologna 2014, 132-135; P Th Camelot. *Introduction*, in Ignace d'Antioche-Policarpe de Smyrne, *Lettres (Sources Chrétiennes)*, Cerf, Paris 1958, 7-61, 47-48; A Jeaubert, *Introduction*, in Clemente, *Epistola ad Corinthios (Sources Chrétiennes*, 167), Cerf, Paris 1971 14-96, 90.

2   Cf. R Repole, *Il Sinodo diocesano. Una prospettiva teologica*, in *Rassegna di Teologia*, 57 (2016/4), 579-603. Cf. also G Routhier *Le Synode diocésain. Le comprendre, le vivre, le célébrer*, Novalis, Ottawa 1995.

Pope's magisterium asks to become reality at many levels and by everyone, with heart, intelligence and will.

Perhaps this is the main challenge for ecclesiology of Francis' teaching.

www.ingramcontent.com/pod-product-compliance
Lightning Source LLC
Chambersburg PA
CBHW052027290426
44112CB00014B/2410